RAINBOWS

FROM HEAVEN

BY:

LYNN ELLEN DOXON

ARTEMESIA PUBLISHING

ROCKY MOUNT, NORTH CAROLINA

Attention corporations, adoption agencies and adoption conferences: Take 40% off and use this book for fundraisers, premiums and gifts. Please contact the publisher:

Artemesia Publishing, LLC
P.O. Box 6508
Rocky Mount, N.C. 27802-6508
252-985-2877
info@artemesiapublishing.com
www.artemesiapublishing.com

Library of Congress Cataloging-in-Publication Data

Doxon, Lynn Ellen
    Rainbows from heaven. / by Lynn Ellen Doxon
        p. cm.
    ISBN 1-932926-98-4 (hardback); 1-932926-99-2 (paperback)
    LCCN: 2004107273

First Printing

Grateful acknowledgement is made to Danny Eversham for permission to reprint exerpts of folk tales fro Carrots to Coins and Other Ukrainian Folk Tales Retold in English by Danny Evanishen, and The Worry Imps and other Ukrainian Folk Tales Retold in English by Danny Evanishen, Box 234, Summerland, BC, V0H 1ZO, danny@ethnic.bc.ca, www.ethnic.bc.ca.

cover by Robert Hursig; cover photo by Kim Jew Photographers; map by Robert Habiger

Acknowledgments

We want to acknowledge International Children's Alliance for helping us complete the adoption. I do not believe any other adoption agency could or would have done what they did. They persevered with us long after they, and we, should have given up. They served us in ways that went way beyond the adoption process. They supported us when we were at our very worst, and when the situation looked the most bleak. We thank them for that.

Our staff and clients at the time of the adoption prayed for us, supported us and took on burdens they had never signed on for without a complaint. We thank Maria, Katrina, Ken and Debbie for shouldering those burdens and remaining friends.

We thank the staff and congregation of St. Stephens United Methodist Church, and the Ukrainian mission team for beginning it, and for seeing it through to the end. They acted as our family in God in every way.

We thank the godparents of the girls, for their prayer, time attention and financial assistance. We couldn't have done it without you, Bob, Jaynie, Nancy, Bob, Steve, and Celeste.

We especially thank my mother, Lydia Doxon, for taking care of all the loose ends and dealing with all the things that needed to be dealt with while we were out of the country and since then, as we were parenting, writing, and working.

And we thank our dear friends in Ukraine, Lana and her family, the entire Malyuta family, Luba and the Svetlanas, and all the others who were our friends and upon whom we depended so heavily while in Ukraine.

For the production of the book, I think Robert for supporting me in every possible way, Anastasia, for answering my many questions about things she would prefer not to remember, Janalyn, for her reviews and comments, and Lydia, for letting Mama work on the book even when she wanted or needed something. I thank Geoff and Beverly for the many ways they have made the book a reality.

To my readers and editors, Betsy Castle, Robyn Martyn, Scott, Heather Wade, Martha Benn, and Jennifer Wilson, thank you for your comments and encouragement.

In addition I would like to thank the small groups I have been a part of at St. Stephens in the years this process has taken place. With the mobility of today's society the group has constantly changed, but the love and support has remained the same.

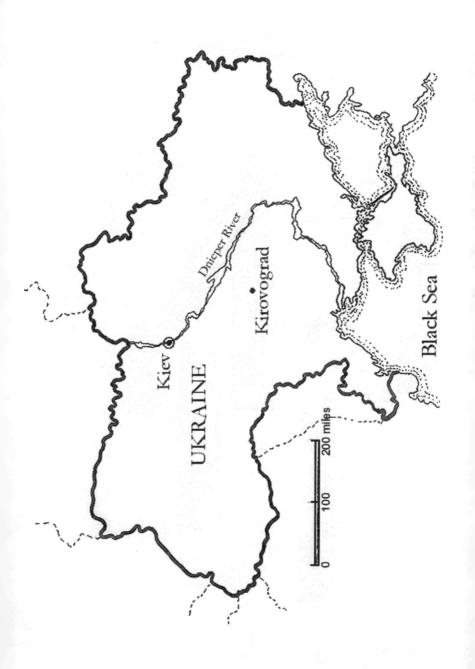

UKRAINE

Kiev

Dnieper River

Kirovograd

Black Sea

0   100   200 miles

v

Dedicated to

Pavlik, Mikhail, and

all the other orphans who didn't make it.

Author's Note:

This is the story of our daughters and how we adopted them. Several of the chapters are told from their point of view. Although the incidents in these chapters are basically accurate, we were relying on the memories of very young children and on things we were told second and third hand to report these incidents. Therefore, those chapters tell more of what might have happened or what could have happened than what really did happen.

Almost everyone we met in Ukraine was named Svetlana, Oksana, Natasha, Irina or Lyudmilla. Therefore many of these people are referred to only by their titles, not their names. Lana is called Lana by all her English-speaking friends, so that is how we knew her, even though her full name is Svetlana Shandruk. The head caretaker in the girls' room at the orphanage is called Sveta even though that is not a nickname the children would have called her. Sveta is a diminutive and would be what an adult would call a child named Svetlana. Our facilitator from Kiev is called Svetlana. In most cases actual names are used (with permission).

Chapter 1

The promise is for you and your children. Acts 2:39a

Anastasia giggled as she dropped the bills into her big sister's hand. She knew this wasn't the proper attitude for begging and that the aged ladies going into the Orthodox church would frown on her behavior, but she didn't care. This was more money than she had ever gotten before in her two and a half years, and she knew that when they had paper money they had always been able to buy a lot of bread. Maybe her sister could even buy a soup bone if Mama didn't find the money first and buy vodka with it. She danced around a little in front of her sister until Svetlana frowned at her and an old *babushka* hit her with her cane. Anastasia returned to the pious position that was acceptable for begging in the little Ukrainian village. Although her head was bent low, she kept glancing sideways at her sister and trying to catch the eye of the men in polished black shoes walking by in hope of getting another large gift. But no one had given her anything else before her sister grabbed her and ran into the church.

"The school truant officer. He is looking for me again. We have to hide. Anastasia, come now!"

They stayed in the church for a really long time, it seemed to Anastasia, then finally slipped out the side entrance and went to the market. As Svetlana bargained for the last two loaves of bread on the shelf, Anastasia played with a bit of string she had found on the floor. Then they started home.

"Can't we get a soup bone so we can have some soup?" she asked.

"Prices have gone up too much. I could barely get two loaves of bread."

1

As they walked, Anastasia kicked at the crisp leaves of the October day. Finally they came around the corner near their little dirt floor hut.

Snijana was playing alone outside the hut. This morning, when Svetlana and Anastasia had left, Mikhail had been there and Mama had been asleep on the floor. They had expected her to sleep for a long time because there had been so many men last night. The men usually brought bottles that Mama drank out of, and then she slept for a long time in the morning.

As Svetlana and Anastasia approached, a big dog ran into the yard. He had a sausage in his mouth that he had probably stolen from somewhere in the village. Snijana saw it and got up, slowly moving closer to the dog. When the dog dropped the sausage, she grabbed it and started to bite it. Suddenly the dog lunged for her. One of its sharp teeth ripping through Snijana's lip. She screamed and rolled over as the dog tried to grab the rest of the sausage. Its jaw locked on her arm and it shook her wildly. Snijana's body went limp.

Svetlana and Anastasia screamed and ran to her, beating the dog with sticks. Neighbors heard the screams and came running. They beat the dog off the tiny girl, who lay in the dirt trembling, and called the police. Police and ambulance soon arrived; finding the fourteen-month-old child unconscious and the other children unattended in a thatch-roofed hut with a dirt floor that contained no food or furniture, only straw-filled pallets and some worn, dirty clothes. Calls had been made about this family before and the policemen knew the reputation of the mother, but things had never been this bad. They called the Education Inspector, who was responsible for the welfare of children in the district. He started proceedings to get all four of the children out of this home. But the first order of business was to get the baby to the hospital.

Mikhail came tearing home from school just as the paramedics loaded Snijana into the ambulance.

"That big dog from down the street attacked Snijana. They are taking her to the hospital. But the ambulance people have called the school truant officer and some other officials. I think they are going to take us away," explained Svetlana. "Why weren't you here? Where is Mama?"

"She got up early this morning. She said she had to go to the clinic. The truant officer came for me right after she left. Snijana was inside, sleeping under a pile of dirty laundry when I left."

"Well she must have come outside after that. Why didn't you lock her in? Mama says to always lock the little ones in when we leave."

"The man wouldn't let me. He was in a hurry, and I couldn't tell him that I had to lock the door because my baby sister was in there, could I?"

Anastasia looked at her brother and sister. Svetlana and Mikhail were the only security she had known in her short life, and they looked worried. That worried Anastasia, too. One of the men told the three of them to get into the car. The three children sat in the back of the car and waited. After a while two men in suits got in the front seat and drove them away. They drove for a long time through the countryside until they came to a city bigger than Anastasia had ever seen. Finally the car pulled into the yard of a big, grey building where several children were doing calisthenics.

Svetlana, Mikhail, and Anastasia followed the man into the building where he talked with a tall woman for a while, then left them. The woman called two other women. One took Mikhail off in one direction, and the other led Anastasia and Svetlana in another. The woman began to comb the girls' hair, carefully inspecting their scalps as she did. Svetlana's was thick, long, and brown and had not been combed in a few days. When the woman was finally through, she led Svetlana out of the room.

Anastasia still had the baby fine hair of a toddler so combing and searching her hair for lice went much faster. Then the woman stripped Anastasia and took her clothes away. She told Anastasia to stand in a dishpan while she poured water over her, then scrubbed her with a soapy washcloth and washed her hair with some bad smelling shampoo that made her eyes sting. Finally the woman poured more water over her, dried her on a rough towel and dressed her in tights, a white undershirt, wool sweater, and flannel skirt.

After her long day, Anastasia was almost asleep. The woman picked her up and carried her into a room where ten other children about her age were sitting around little tables. She put Anastasia down and told her to sit in the chair. Anastasia joined two girls and a boy at one little table. One of the girls kicked her under the table, and she kicked back, glaring at the girl. Then someone poured broth into the teacup in front of her. They ladled in a quarter of a potato. So, she would get soup after all tonight. She wondered where Svetlana and Mikhail were, but not for long. She was soon totally absorbed in eating her soup and the thick slice of bread they had given her.

After the meal, the brown-eyed woman who had served them took the plates, cups, and spoons away and turned the television on. Anastasia had never seen television before. Someone was inside the little box, singing a song. "How could anyone fit in that little box?" Anastasia asked the woman who had served her meal. The woman said "Shhh." When she turned to the other children, they looked at her with frightened eyes and shook their heads. She settled back on the floor and was soon asleep.

Someone shook Anastasia awake. At first she was disoriented. Then, as a woman put her on her feet and led her to the bathroom, she remembered where she was and what had happened today. In the bathroom everyone sat on little pots until they had gone to the bathroom. Then they went back to the eating room, picked up their chairs and were led to another room with beds lined up all in a row. Anastasia copied the girl who had kicked her. The woman showed Anastasia how to lay her clothes on the chair at the foot of her bed. She put on the pajamas she found under her pillow and climbed into bed. But when the lights were turned out she could not go to sleep. She lay awake, feeling lonely and frightened, wondering where her sisters and brother were. She had never slept in a bed or by herself before. Finally she fell into a deep sleep and woke the next day to rain drumming on the windows and a woman loudly ordering everyone out of bed.

After a trip to the bathroom Anastasia had to dress herself and comb her own hair. This was the first time she had ever combed her own hair, and she got the comb tangled in it. Finally one of the women came to help and braided her hair in two braids. Anastasia looked at herself in the mirror as she was leaving the room. The braids looked really cute. She would ask them to braid her hair every day. She skipped into the other room, just like Svetlana had been trying to teach her.

Snijana lay in the hospital bed shaking with fright as the men looked at her face. At fourteen months all she knew was that she hurt, she was afraid, and Anastasia and Mikhail, who always protected her, were not there. They put a mask over her face, and she began to smell a suffocating smell. She struggled but was soon asleep. When she woke, she started to cry but her lip hurt so much she couldn't. Her upper lip was so swollen that she couldn't

5

eat, and it was difficult to sip the broth they fed her. Her arm hurt, too. Kind ladies came in often to check on her and a very gentle doctor examined her. They fed her broth, and when she could eat it, mashed potatoes, then bread. Between visits she lay huddled in the corner of the hospital crib trying not to cry because it would hurt her lip.

Snijana was beginning to feel comfortable with the hospital routine and the nice ladies who helped her there. Then another woman in a grey dress came and took her to a little room where they washed her and dressed her in warm clothes. The nice ladies at the hospital hugged her and said good-bye as the woman in the grey dress carried her out. The woman put her in the back of the car and told her to stay there while she went back in to get some papers. Snijana sat there for a long time shivering before the lady came back with the papers and started the car. They drove to a long yellow brick build-ing and the lady took her to a room full of children. There was Anastasia! They held each other, so glad to see each other after the first separation of their lives.

"Where have you been?" Anastasia asked.

"Hothpito," said Snijana.

"I don't know where Svetlana and Mikhail are," Anastasia whispered. "They led them away and I haven't seen them since."

The woman in charge of the room called them to come eat. Lunch was a bowl full of soup with a potato in it. Snijana really liked having a full bowl of soup and a potato. She smiled at the lady, but the lady didn't smile back. It still hurt a little to smile.

Soon, life in this place with the other kids and all the different women who came to take care of them seemed normal. There were lots of rules and a very strict routine. Anastasia told Snijana she had to smile to get what she wanted. When Snijana smiled, it was as though the sun had come out. And when she smiled, the women were very nice to Snijana, and she felt safe. And if that didn't work, Mikhail and Svetlana had taught her long ago how to take things she wanted when no one was looking. Then one day, a woman in a white coat came, put them into a car and drove them away. They drove for hours along snowy roads with forests and fields on either side. The car seemed to rock back and forth, making Snijana feel a little sick. Trees flew by, making her feel even worse. The woman drove awfully fast, and while she drove she waved her hands around and told them stories of witches and wolves, who lived in the forest. Snijana was so frightened tears began to slip down her cheeks, but she had already learned that she could be hit if she cried out loud, so she cried silently.

After their long drive, they came to another big building, but this one was nicer than the one where they had been living for the past two months. They walked in behind the lady, Anastasia holding Snijana's hand protectively. The woman left them in a room just inside the door. Another woman, with funny orange hair, told them to take off all their clothes. The lady who had brought them took the clothes and left. Again they were inspected for lice. Snijana's mind kept seeing wolves with big yellow teeth come toward her out of the forest the whole time the woman was washing her. Then the woman got out a needle and syringe and gave them each three shots. Anastasia pinched herself to keep from crying out. Tears came to Snijana's eyes but she did not cry. They slipped into the underwear and undershirts the new orphanage provided and the nice lady helped them put on tights, skirts, and sweaters. Snijana smiled at her, and the woman smiled back. She liked that. At least one of the people in this place could smile.

When they were clean and dressed, the lady made some calls on the telephone. Two other women came. One took Anastasia away down the hall. Snijana tried to run after her, but the other woman held her back. Svetlana had been led away, and they had never seen her again. What if she didn't ever get to see Anastasia again?

Chapter 2

I tell you the truth, whatever you did for one of these, the least of these brothers of mine, you did for me. Matthew 25:40

"Please, may I buy it?" asked William.

"You may choose one thing," I told him. We were at a silent auction to raise money for the mission team our church, St. Stephen's United Methodist, was sending to Ukraine in the summer. Members of the congregation had donated all sorts of items, and they had a special child's table, with less expensive items.

"Allison, have you decided on anything?" I asked the quiet ten-year-old at my side.

"I want something pretty," she said.

"Look at this little doll. It is pretty, isn't it?"

"Oh, yes. Can I bid on it?"

"Sure you can," I assured her. "Where is Alexandra?"

"I think she went downstairs," William told me. "She finished her bidding a long time ago."

I went in search of the youngest of our three foster children. They were not used to getting to choose things on their own and were each handling it in their own way. Eleven-year-old William couldn't decide because he wanted everything. Ten-year-old Allison didn't know what she wanted. Alexandra, at seven, knew what she wanted and let others know about it, but then disappeared to avoid the potential consequences of being so bold.

My husband Robert and I rounded up the kids and went into the benefit concert that was part of the fundraiser. The kids had already gorged on a spaghetti dinner and ice cream, so they were content to sit through the concert by the music director of the church.

"I wish I could go," I whispered to Robert.

"You aren't an English teacher. Besides, what would we do with the kids? Sam can't find respite care for three weeks. She can barely manage to find a place for us to leave the kids for a three-day weekend."

In late 1994, when I overheard our pastor Steve Martyn talking to Betsy Castle, an English teacher and member of the mission committee, one night after a women's group meeting my ears immediately perked up. A group called International Institute for Christian Studies or IICS was looking for a team of teachers to go to Ukraine to teach American English to Ukrainian English teachers. In addition to English, they would be teaching Bible studies. They would leave just after school was out the following June. Immediately, I rushed home and told Robert, about it. He was intrigued, too, but neither of us could see a place for us on the mission team. He is an architect who specializes in church design and consulting, mostly Roman Catholic churches, and I have a degree in horticulture and write a gardening column for the local paper.

Betsy, a slender, energetic, goal-oriented person, went to work creating a team right away. She and her husband Rich Castle, a retired Air Force Colonel who had been stationed in Europe with NATO for several years, put together a team of nine people. It was quite an undertaking for our 350-member church, but we had been stretching farther in the last few years. As pastor Steve Martyn had placed greater emphasis on spiritual formation, and as members of the church grew spiritually, we took on greater and greater challenges. This mission trip was just one of a variety of new projects and programs that were springing up in the church.

Part of the team would stay in Kiev, and the other members would teach American English to English teachers at School # 11 in Kirovograd, Ukraine, a rural district that had had even fewer Western visitors than Kiev.

I was fascinated by the part of the world the St. Stepehns team would be traveling to. As I learned more I discovered that there are many parallels between New Mexico and Kirovograd. Kirovograd, like New Mexico, is close to a region of granite outcrops that are rich in uranium ore. Kirovograd was a major weapon-manufacturing region during the Communist Era. The region was completely closed to foreign visitors, and security was very tight. Even after the fall of Communism, some parts of the region were not open to foreign visitors, and many of the people were distrustful of foreigners, especially Americans.

The Kirovograd region is less densely populated than most of Ukraine, and is predominantly rural, like New Mexico. There are many deposits of ores of precious metals, and several mineral springs where Eastern Europeans come for baths. They consider their high radon levels excellent for "relaxation cures" while we consider ours somewhat dangerous. Both Kirovograd and New Mexico are home to ancient civilizations, although theirs are somewhat older than ours. A house made of mastodon bones, found in Ukraine but not in the Kirovograd region, is the oldest human house ever found.

The Tuesday after the fundraising dinner the girls came home from school. First I checked to make sure Alexandra hadn't thrown her homework in the gutter again, then I asked, "Where is William?"

"He wasn't on the bus," volunteered Alexandra.

"Allison, did you see him?"

"I don't know."

"You have to walk down the same hallway he does after school. Did you see him in the hallway?"

"Yes."

"Did you see him at the bus stop?"

"Yes. But then he went away."

"Did he say where he was going?"

"No."

I called the school; the principal answered. She said she would check with his teacher in the older kids special education class. The teacher reported that he had gotten to the bus stop. Teachers searched the school while the principal called the bus driver. I loaded the girls in the car and drove the bus route in reverse order to see if he had gotten off at the wrong stop. We stopped to talk with some of Alexandra's friends at a park that was one of the bus stops, but they didn't recall seeing him. We didn't find him anywhere. When we got to the school, the principal said the bus driver did not remember seeing him. He had disappeared sometime between the time his teacher left him at the bus stop and the bus driver picked them up. It was now over an hour since school had gotten out. Time to call Human Services.

"Hello, is Samantha Garcia there?" I asked.

"She is not available at the moment," the receptionist said.

"Could I talk with Mr. Thomas? This is Lynn Doxon calling about a missing foster child."

Mr. Thomas was the department head.

When I explained what had happened, he told me he would alert Sam and gave me a list of nighttime emergency numbers.

Just after I had hung up the school principal called.

"William is here," she said. "He tried to walk home but went in the wrong direction. Fortunately he found his way back to the school."

When Sam called, I was able to tell her that William was found, then I rushed down to the school to pick him up.

"I got tired of waiting," he told me. "I thought I could get home faster by walking, because we are the last stop and riding the bus is boring."

"But you didn't know the way home," I protested. "What made you go the way you did?"

"I could see the tall building where Sam's office is," he said. "I knew that was not too far from our house, so I walked toward it. But when I got there I didn't know which way to go to get to our house from there, so I just went back to the school. That was easy, because I just had to walk away from the tall building."

"Even if you walked in a straight line you had to have walked over four miles. If you were at Sam's office, why didn't you go in and ask someone to call us?"

"I forgot what floor her office was on. Could I please have something to drink?"

About two weeks later I got a call from Sam.

"We have the results back from the review team in Santa Fe. We have a therapeutic foster home for William in the South Valley and a place for the girls in Los Lunas."

"You are taking the girls? Why are you taking the girls?"

"The board in Santa Fe reviewed all the three and decided that it would be best for all three of them to be in therapeutic foster homes. Nobody could handle all three of them, so we are sending the girls to one home and William to another."

"I have been handling all three for the last six months."

"Yes, and we are grateful for that."

"But I have told you we want to adopt the girls. Why do you have to take them away from us?"

"We thought it would be better to move all of them at once, rather than make William think there is something wrong with him because we moved him."

"William is schizophrenic. The doctor explained the diagnosis to him the last time he was there. He knows that there is something wrong. But the girls don't need therapeutic foster care."

"You said you had to re-teach Allison how to use the broom every time you want her to sweep the floor."

"She needs special education, yes, but not therapeutic foster care."

"And what about Alexandra. She can't sit still for five minutes."

"We had her tested. She is not hyperactive, just hyper vigilant. That is because for most of her life she has been the only one who knows what is going on. She is the memory for the whole family. That is quite a burden for a seven-year-old. She has been in thirteen different schools in kindergarten and first grade and still reads at grade level. That proves she can learn. Why do you have to take the girls? Why can't we adopt them?"

"There is no plan to release them for adoption."

"But you know their mother will never be able to take care of them. Why can they not be released?"

"It is our policy to reunite families whenever possible."

"That is not going to happen in this case, and these children are going to be in foster care all their lives. Less than one percent of kids get adopted in New Mexico. The rest of them get sent back to their families to be abused again and again. Why?"

"Our policy is reunification. I am just a social worker. I don't set policy."

"Sam, are we ever going to get to adopt kids in New Mexico?"

"Right now all of the kids we have available are Hispanic kids."

"Isn't it better for a Hispanic kid to have a home with loving non-Hispanic parents than to not have a home at all?"

"Our policy is that Hispanic kids go to Hispanic parents."

"O.K. But you are going to tell the kids they are moving."

"I will. When do you think you will be ready to take some more kids?"

"Don't talk to me about that right now. Every child you have sent us has ended up going to therapeutic foster care, where the parents get paid $30,000 a year to do what I have been dong for $3000. And you told us that taking foster kids was the best way to get a child we could eventually adopt."

"Well, the policy keeps changing. And you are one of the best. We need you. We don't have very many foster parents who are as well educated, as caring and as dedicated as you. Will you at least take emergency placements until you are ready for a permanent placement?"

"I suppose so. But I still feel used."

That night I had the dream again. Two little girls were kneeling at the altar rail at our church, and they were mine. I knew they were mine. They knelt at the rail with their back to me. Or was it three little girls? I really couldn't tell.

William, Allison, and Alexandra were taken out of the house in April.

Members of the St. Stephen's youth group each had secret prayer partners throughout that year. The identity of the secret prayer partners was revealed at a dinner in mid June. However, Robert's prayer partner was Jude Machin, a high school junior and the youngest member of the Ukraine Mission Team. He would be in Ukraine and miss the dinner. Robert called Jude a few days before the team left, telling him that he had been praying for him all year and had watched his preparation for the Ukraine trip with great interest. Jude told Robert he needed a few more things to take to Ukraine, so Robert collected several of the things. On the day they left, we went to the airport to see them off. Jude had excelled in Russian in school and was eager to practice but was also very nervous about this significant test of his ability.

While the mission team was in the Ukraine we continued to pray for them. We were all eager to hear about the trip when they returned. One Saturday evening after the team's return they presented a slide show about the trip.

"School #11 specializes in teaching English." Betsy informed us during the slide show. "However, in addition to the regular school, where students in grades one through eleven study the traditional Ukrainian curriculum, Margarita, the director of School #11, started several satellite schools in houses she had purchased in the neighborhood. In each school twenty to thirty students in the same grade spend the day with a teacher, a monitor, and a cook, and caretaker. Half the day the students study from an American Christian home school curriculum, starting right out in English on the first day of first grade. The other half of the day they study the things they will need to know to pass the standardized Ukrainian tests. By third grade most of these children are quite proficient in English. Their parents pay an extra fee for the children to go to these schools, so they are attended by students from wealthy families.

"Most of the teachers are Christian and see this as a way to combat a-moral lifestyles and organized crime in their city. The teachers in these small satellite schools, who are the best English speakers, studied with the mission team and were very receptive to the Bible studies we led, even acting as evangelists among the other teachers. The newest teacher among these satellite schoolteachers was assigned to be the interpreter and guide for the mission team. Her name is Lana.

"One day Lana asked Glenda Ehrig and me if we would like to visit an orphanage near her home. Lana's mother and she had volunteered at the orphanage over the years. Glenda and I saw a great need at the orphanage. Although the adult caregivers were loving and professional, the orphanage facility itself needed repairs. We decided to take the men on the team to visit the orphanage. When the entire team visited we decided to give the director our undesignated mission money to spruce up the playground. When we gave it to her the director exclaimed, 'How wonderful! Now the children can have some milk and fresh fruit!'"

The orphanage touched the team members, and they took many pictures of the tiny abandoned babies and the young children playing. "This orphanage was only for children less than four years of age, and there were 150 children in it." Betsy said. "More children are increasingly being abandoned in orphanages because their parents cannot afford to care for them. Sometimes the parents will leave the children in the orphanage for the first four years of their lives, then take them home. Sometimes they are abandoned forever. A child with any type of birth defect was very likely to be abandoned. This orphanage had been established for children with mental disabilities but now houses more abandoned children than anything else."

After the presentation Betsy approached me with a picture of a dark skinned girl with a red bow in her hair. "Her name is Violetta," Betsy said. "She will not be adopted by anyone in Ukraine because she is half gypsy and half black. Very few adoptions are taking place in Ukraine now and there is almost no chance for Violetta, even though she is one of the most intelligent, well-liked girls in the orphanage."

I knew instantly that I wanted to adopt her. What I didn't know was that Betsy had talked with Robert, too, and he had the same feeling.

Foreign adoptions had been halted in Ukraine in 1994 after a scandal involving illegal adoptions, in which a doctor provided babies to foreigners for very high fees, not always with the consent of the mother. By 1995 new laws had been passed for international adoptions but the system for completing these adoptions was not entirely in place.

At School #11, Rich and Betsy had met Anya Malyuta and her twin sister Julia. Both had applied for an exchange program in the United States. Her sister had been selected but Anya had not, so Rich and Betsy agreed to host her for a year. The connection with this family would prove to be very valuable for us.

We had no idea how to accomplish the adoption. We checked the United States Department of State adoption web site for information on Ukraine, but it wasn't very helpful because the laws were so new and the procedures not developed. We contacted Rainbow House, a local international adoption agency in Albuquerque, but they said they didn't have any contacts in Ukraine and couldn't really help us. Finally Betsy suggested that Anya could call the Ministry of Education in Ukraine for us. Because it is nine hours later in Ukraine than in New Mexico, Betsy and Anya got up at 5:00 one weekday and came over to our house. Betsy was her usual chipper self, but Anya was not quite awake yet. I handed her a list of questions to ask.

"The most important thing is to get a complete list of procedures to follow," I told her.

Betsy dialed the number and handed the phone to Anya. Eventually she was connected to the right person and started asking my questions. She wrote out the answers to the questions as fast as she could. Betsy and I read the answers as she wrote.

"What does that mean?" I asked.

"Do they need more than one copy?" asked Betsy.

"How should this request to adopt Violetta be worded?"

Just as Anya would get one answer half written, Betsy or I would fire off another question. While we were asking questions on one side, the person at the Ministry of Education was asking questions on the other side. Anya did a truly admirable job of translating from English to Ukrainian, Ukrainian to English and writing answers all at the same time, although by the time she finished she was nearly in tears. She thanked them for their help, they complimented her for having such a good Ukrainian accent for an American student, and she hung up. Her notes included a list of twelve documents we would need. These were a home study, a marriage certificate, proof of income, police clearance, health certificates for each of us, proof of citizenship, an application to adopt Violetta, commitment to register her with the Ukrainian Embassy in the United States and provide annual reports for three years, copies of our passports, and a valid entrance permit for an adopted child into the Untied States. The application was not a form to be filled out. We had to write a statement describing what we wanted to do. We later learned that the statement had to meet the requirements of the particular official to whom it was submitted but would not necessarily be accepted as it was by the next official.

We hired Rainbow House to do a home study and follow-up reports and to help us in any way they could. Rosalind, the social worker there, was very sympathetic and helpful through the whole process, which turned out to be much more of a process than we anticipated.

We needed a statement from the bank saying how secure our deposits were and how much money we usually kept there. The bank would not give us a letter so we changed banks to a friendlier, helpful institution. Our new bank accountant wrote a letter saying that we owned our own business and that it was expected to be successful for the next several years. In the United States, income tax returns are generally used to show income and financial security. In Ukraine there was so much cheating on taxes and the government was so weak that government forms were not considered reliable sources of information. A letter from a bank official, however, was considered reliable.

When we had all the documents, they had to be translated into Ukrainian. I called the University of New Mexico.

The head of the Russian Department said, "We have several Russian translators. Russian is widely spoken in Ukraine. Can it be translated into

Russian?"

"No," I said. "The official language is Ukrainian. Even if they do understand Russian, it has to be in Ukrainian."

"We'll see what we can do."

A few days later a professor who was on sabbatical called me.

"There is one woman who might be able to do the translations you are looking for. Her name is Lyudmilla. She is a student here."

Lyudmilla lived in a retirement home next to the Jewish Community Center with her husband. As she translated the documents that revealed everything about our lives, she told me about her life. In Ukraine, when it had been part of the Soviet Union, she had worked as a medical technician and later dean of students at a university. Lyudmilla and her husband had both been able to immigrate to the United States under a special Jewish refugee program because he was Jewish, although she wasn't. Things weren't going too well with her husband, so even though she was in her sixties she was studying nutrition at the University of New Mexico, hoping to get a job.

She had applied for American citizenship and was trying to earn enough money to bring her son and his wife to the United States. We met several times to work out the exact meaning and purpose of the documents. She talked about how things had been in Ukraine in the Soviet Union, then in Ukraine after 1991, when Ukraine became independent. On one visit she said people tended to believe whatever the government told them and that they had been very surprised to learn that much of it was not true when the Soviet Union collapsed. She also warned me not to give Violetta too much rich food when she first came. When she and her husband had first arrived, she had immediately bought all sorts of food at the supermarket, but they got sick from it. When she had discovered the health food market and started buying things they were used to eating, their health improved.

Throughout that fall and winter, more foster children came to us, often in the middle of the night, covered with bruises or suffering from flu or head lice. They poured soap bubbles in our aquarium, hid out in their rooms or tried to run away to get back to their friends. They were usually gone within three days. We had one voluntary placement. Her father had just died, her older sister had run away, and her mother had called the Children Youth and Families Department and said she couldn't cope and was afraid of what she would do. The other thirty or so foster children arrived with the police.

Every Sunday I would stare at Violetta's picture on the Missions bulletin board at St. Stephen's United Methodist Church, where the pictures from the previous summer were still on display. I was trying to memorize everything about Violetta. One day Robert came up behind me.

"Look at that cute little blonde with the big smile," I said. "Isn't she adorable?"

"She is," said Robert. "She looks like she has spirit, too."

"If anything prevents us from adopting Violetta, we should try to adopt the girl with the blue bow."

Chapter 3

From the lips of infants and children you have ordained praise. Psalm 8:2a

Natasha held up the coat again and showed the children how to button the buttons. Pavlik had figured it out the second time he was shown, but Anastasia just couldn't seem to get the hang of it. She watched once more. Natasha made it look so simple, but to Anastasia's little three-year-old fingers it was really hard to get the button through the buttonhole. She tried one more time, but her scarf got in the way.

"Push it with your thumb," whispered Pavlik.

Anastasia pushed and the button finally slipped through the buttonhole. She laughed and showed Natasha. Natasha hugged her. Anastasia loved Natasha more than any other caregiver.

Anastasia and Pavlik were excited. They were going out in the snow. They seldom got to go outside if it was snowing. They might get sick. It was really bad to get sick. A child who had to go to the hospital would probably not come back to the orphanage. That had happened to one of their friends.

Outside, finally, Pavlik said to Anastasia, "Let's pretend you are my sister."

"O.K.," said Anastasia. "And pretend we have a mother."

"And a father," said Pavlik.

"Mother is going to the market to get us a soup bone and some cabbage," said Anastasia.

"And some milk," said Pavlik.

"You don't get milk from the market, you get milk from the milk truck on the corner," said Anastasia.

23

"Oh, I have never been to the market," said Pavlik.

"There are lots of wooden boxes," she said. "With people behind them. You go and talk to the people, then you shout for a while, and finally you get a soup bone to put in your bag."

In the snow they marked out the space for their market and made the other kids act as shopkeepers. Anastasia told each of them what to sell and how to sell it. When the other children tired of playing market, Anastasia and Pavlik went to the side of the yard under a tree, which had become their own special place. There they laid out their house and yard, pretending to grow fruits and vegetables in the yard and chasing after imaginary chickens.

They played brother and sister for a while longer then Natasha called them to get in line. As they lined up, Anastasia saw Snijana coming out with her group. This was the only time they saw each other anymore, when they were coming or going to play time or music, but at least she knew Snijana was still in the orphanage. Sometimes, during music, they got to sit together. Then she would hold Snijana on her lap and help her with the songs.

All in a line, the twelve three and four-year-olds marched back into the orphanage, up the stairs, and into the cloakroom that opened off the hall in the far corner of the big building. They took off their identical coats, hung them with their identical scarves and hats in their little closets, and put their boots carefully on the floor. When all the children had their outdoor clothing hung up and their indoor slippers on, they filed into the day room, where they ate, did lessons, and played most of the day. When they were sitting in the two rows of chairs facing each other, their lessons began.

Sveta took an apple out of her big black bag. "What is this?" she asked.

"*Yablaka*," they said in unison.

Each child repeated the word for apple as Sveta corrected their pronunciation.

"What is this?" she asked, pulling out a potato.

"That is a shriveled up old clod," giggled Anastasia. The other children giggled with her.

"That is quite enough, young lady," exclaimed Sveta. "You take your chair and go sit in that corner."

Anastasia picked up her chair and carried it to the corner. On the way she looked at Natasha who hid a little smirk behind her hand. The potato was a bit shriveled.

The lesson on fruits and vegetables continued for about half an hour before Sveta got out a book and read a fairy tale about three goats and a bridge. This was Anastasia's favorite so she sat quietly listening.

When lessons were over, Anastasia was allowed to get out of her chair and play with the other children on the floor. Anastasia had another idea for a game. Today Pavlik was the Papa and Anastasia was the Mama. Mama swept the floor while she told Papa that he needed to go out and find a decent job so he could support the family. Pavlik said he would just leave if she was going to treat him that way. Anastasia started crying real tears. As he comforted her, Pavlik said he would never leave her and promised that they would grow up together and he would marry her when they were old enough.

They sat together holding hands at lunch. Anastasia was really hungry after playing outside in the snow. But the soup was really watery, there wasn't any extra bread, and they hadn't had fruit all week. The food was getting worse and worse, and she didn't like it. When she had first come to the orphanage, the food had been much better and more plentiful. What was going on now? If she complained they would probably send her to bed without anything, so she kept her mouth shut and ate what they gave her, but in between bites she made faces at Pavlik. The girl across the table laughed at her, spitting her food all over the table. Sveta slapped the girl across the face and scolded her. Anastasia was sorry she had made her laugh and quit making the faces.

After lunch Anastasia and Pavlik filed into the sleeping room behind the other children. Pavlik took off his pants and hung them over the foot of his bed, then put his sweater on top of them. Anastasia did the same with her skirt and sweater. Both Pavlik and Anastasia considered naptime a waste of time, but they had learned to lie quietly for the hour and a half in order to avoid punishment. They were best friends. Anastasia knew they would get married when they grew up and that made her feel content and cheerful.

When naptime was finally over and they could go into the day room again for more lessons, they sat at the tables and Sveta passed around books. The girl who had laughed at Anastasia's faces got Anastasia's favorite book. Anastasia let her keep it to make up for getting her in trouble. Instead Anastasia took the book about Thumbelina from the boy across from her and gave him the book about the giant she had been given. She did not like to look at pictures of giants, wolves, or monsters.

Chapter 4

We are therefore Christ's ambassadors, as though God were making his appeal through us. 2 Corinthians 5:20

In January the second Ukraine mission team started meeting together during the Sunday School hour. I was the only new member of the team. Three members of the team were going to Kiev and five to Kirovograd. Jude Machin and Betsy and Rich Castle would all be going to Kirovograd again. Steve Roberts, a postal worker with a degree in theology, would be our spiritual leader. I felt uncertain and wanted to know more about where we would be going and what we would be doing, but I didn't even know what questions to ask.

"What do they want to know?" I asked Betsy.

"What they really want to know is English. You can teach them some horticulture words they wouldn't learn otherwise."

"How will it work?"

"Your horticulture class will last five days. The second and third weeks you will repeat the course with different students. After teaching for two hours, you will have a break. Then you will teach English as a Second Language classes and Bible study. Your class for this part of the study will be the same for all three weeks, so you will get to know the teachers better and be able to go into more depth with the Bible Study. So you need to prepare fifteen days of Bible study."

Every week Rich reported on the progress toward getting visas, airline tickets, and other logistics; asked about our fundraising efforts; and talked about the Ukrainian culture. Betsy helped us prepare English as a Second

27

Language lessons.

I decided that on the first day of the horticulture course we would take a walk and learn the common names of the plants we saw. I would start by explaining that there could be more than one common name for a plant but only one scientific name. The second day I would talk about Robert's and my house in New Mexico and the landscaping around it. For the third and fourth day I created a simple business game, like one played by American high school economics students. On the final day I would answer questions and discuss anything they wanted to talk about. Through the whole preparation period I was a little ambivalent about the exact goal of the teaching. The other members of the team assured me that the primary goal was an opportunity to learn new words and American-style English.

I was even more hesitant about preparing my Bible Study. We were studying the minor prophets in my Bible Study Fellowship class, but I didn't think that would be the best introduction to the Bible for people raised under Communist rule. One evening as I was meditating on what to teach, Paul's letter to the Ephesians popped into my mind. When I mentioned this at church, several people affirmed my decision and gave me study guides on Ephesians. As I planned the study, I could see how it could easily fall into a three-week study. I would emphasize love and unity the first week, ways we should live the second week with family relationships, and the armor of God the third week.

Lyudmilla started coming to St. Stephens. She made friends in the Senior Fellowship and several of the members began helping her. Her husband had divorced her to marry a Jewish woman whom he had met at the retirement home, leaving her almost penniless and with questionable legal status. She was studying hard to pass the citizenship test.

"Children are very important in Ukraine," she told us. "We take good care of our children. You will find that Violetta has been loved, even in the orphanage."

We didn't think Violetta could be as hurt as some of the foster children we had cared for. She had been in one place since she was abandoned at birth, and the orphanage was well staffed, so she had been adequately taken care of.

Almost weekly someone approached Robert and me, telling us that adopting from Eastern Europe was a mistake. They told us the orphanages there were horrible, that the children would have attachment disorder or any number of other problems. This didn't bother Robert, but I began to wonder what the children might have been through. One of the reasons we weren't adopting in the United States was because so many of the available children have experienced traumatic events that have left them with lasting psychological scars. Because of our experience with special needs foster children, we knew how to handle psychologically damaged children, but after dealing with adolescents and pre-adolescents with multiple personalities, mental retardation, and schizophrenia, I wanted relatively healthy children. I asked the Missions team what the orphanage had been like.

"They were very loving and tender toward the children," Betsy told me. "The children seemed healthy and happy."

"Steve really liked the babies," Jude told me. "There was one baby he just wouldn't put down."

Steve smiled at the memory. "She was very quiet; didn't cry like some of the others. But she had the most intensely intelligent hazel eyes, and she just stared straight into my eyes the entire time I held her. Her name was Irina. They said she had been brought straight from the hospital to the orphanage. I don't think she got a lot of attention. She was in the room where they keep the older infants, not the newborns, so she had to be six or seven months old, but she was very small."

"It is very difficult for Luba, the orphanage director, to get enough to feed them, so they may have some nutritional deficiencies. They don't have enough milk, so they stop giving them milk at about eighteen months," Betsy told us.

There were a few things we were not sure about or did not understand in the instructions for preparing the adoption documents. We really wanted to make sure everything was right, so we asked Anya to make another phone call to the Ministry of Education. This time, before we called, she told us, "No questions while I am on the phone. Write out all your questions ahead of time, then you have to be quiet while I am talking."

We agreed not to interrupt her and to listen quietly. The only new information we got from that call was that we would need three copies of everything. I still had no idea what to do once I got to Ukraine with all our documents. Since there had been no foreign adoptions in Ukraine in two years, apparently there were no procedures to follow.

At St. Stephens members were gathering gifts for us to give to people in Ukraine. Several doctors in the congregation were concerned that medical supplies and medicines were not available in Ukraine. They talked to pharmaceutical companies and collected antibiotic samples and outdated surgical packs for the orphanage and the hospital where Anya's father was a pediatric surgeon. At Dr. Malyta's hospital they often used the same supposedly disposable scalpel or syringe for weeks or even months at a time. Other church friends gave us cosmetic samples, silk scarves, and small gifts to hand out.

In early spring we had all the money we needed. We got our visas and airline tickets. The course material was prepared. Except for the document-ation for the adoption, everything was ready for the trip to Ukraine. My life became centered around the completion of the documents. I made phone calls, filled out forms, and badgered all the people who hadn't returned the necessary documents. Finally, at the end of May, we had every-thing but the U.S. entry visa for Violetta. Rosalind, our social worker, sug-gested that we get permission to bring two children into the country. She said, "You never can tell what may happen once you get to Ukraine." When we got the visa, everything had to be sealed by the State of New Mexico Secretary of State, the United States State Department, and the Ukrainian Embassy. I copied everything and took three unsealed copies with me. Robert would get the necessary seals before he came over to complete the adoption process.

Chapter 5

...the unfading beauty of a gentle and quiet spirit, which is of great worth in God's sight. 1 Peter 3:4

Snijana was so excited. The girls were getting dressed up in the pretty embroidered dresses with flowers in their hair. That meant someone was coming to visit the orphanage. The only time they got dressed up in these costumes was when they were doing a program or someone was visiting. They hadn't been practicing a program so it must be visitors. When everyone was ready, they lined up and walked to the big music room with the mural of the woods at the end. Anastasia was there. Snijana got out of her line and went to hug Anastasia. Vera told her to get back in line. Anastasia was whispering with that boy she played with all the time. Why could she do things that were bad and not get in trouble, but Snijana got in trouble every time she did one little thing?

A man came into the room with Luba, followed by two other men and a woman. A man with a camera followed them.

"Boys and girls," Luba said, "this is the mayor of Kirovograd. He is here to have some pictures taken with you. These people are going to make a brochure about the city, and they want pictures of our model orphanage in the brochure."

The photographer looked at the children. "Let's have her and her and her," he said. Anastasia was one of the first to be chosen. Anastasia was always first to be chosen. Then the photographer turned to Snijana's group. Snijana smiled her prettiest smile.

"Let's include this one," he said, pointing to Snijana. "She is about the prettiest little thing I have ever seen. Stand there. Very good. No, wait. We need a boy. You!" he said, pointing at Anastasia. "We don't need you. Get that boy over here."

They took lots of pictures, until Snijana was really tired of smiling and standing with the others.

Anastasia made faces at Snijana. Anastasia made faces like that any time Snijana got something that Anastasia didn't. But Anastasia always watched really closely to make sure none of the caregivers were looking, and she never got caught. Snijana had never seen Anastasia get caught doing anything. Snijana was so jealous of the things Anastasia could get away with that she wanted to hit her. But then Snijana would get punished and Anastasia would not. She hung her head and wrinkled her nose.

When the picture taking was over, they went back to their rooms and put on the matching rompers they usually wore in the spring. As Snijana was putting hers on, she noticed a little rip in the side. She stuck her foot into the romper leg and her toe got caught in the little hole. The whole side ripped out. Snijana froze. Sure enough, Vera had noticed the ripping sound.

"Snijana Mikhailovna, what have you done now?"

Snijana dropped the rompers. She made her mind go empty so she would not feel the spanking she knew was coming. She hoped it was only a spanking this time. Nobody seemed to like to hurt kids as much as Vera, and she seemed to take special pleasure in punishing Snijana. Vera had only been working there a little while but she had already beaten Snijana twice. As Vera raised her hand to beat Snijana, Luba walked in.

"Get out," she ordered Vera. "I will not have children beaten in my orphanage. You may leave immediately."

Snijana let go of the blankness and smiled at Luba who picked her up and hugged her.

"I tore the clothes," Snijana said in a tiny voice.

Luba sighed. "Everything is wearing out," she said. "It is warm today. Everyone take off your rompers and go to music in your panties and shirts. Julia, take them to music," she ordered as she picked up the torn and frayed rompers.

"Please," said Snijana in her tiniest voice. "Could I go to the bathroom first?"

All the children followed Julia to the bathroom for their morning potty break.

Then Julia led the way to the music room where Lyudmilla and the other group of two and three year olds was waiting for them. Music was Snijana's favorite part of the day. Lyudmilla sometimes let her play the keys on the piano, too. She smiled as pretty as she could for Lyudmilla.

"Today we are going to start practicing a special May Day program, boys and girls." Lyudmilla said. "Snijana, I want you to be the fox and you three boys will be the rabbits."

Snijana stepped forward, beaming. This would be fun. Foxes were clever and quick and not afraid of anything, not even mean ladies who liked to hit little kids. They could outsmart dogs who tried to chase them. Yes, Snijana would like to be a fox.

Chapter 6

"You did not choose me, but I chose you and appointed you to go and bear fruit -- fruit that would last. Then the father will give you whatever you ask in my name. John 15:16

We left the first week in June. Anya's sister, Julia, quit her student exchange program early to make it back to Ukraine in time to graduate with their class. Julia joined us in Amsterdam. The only international flights I had been on before were to Canada and Central America, which are mere hops compared to flying to Europe. This flight seemed to last forever. I visited with other members of the team and other passengers and watched the movie *Mr. Holland's Opus* during the flight, but mostly I struggled with how I would be able to handle the adoption process without Robert. I hadn't slept on the flight across the Atlantic, so I was tired and disoriented when we landed in Amsterdam. We had plenty of time between our flights, so we walked stowed our bags in a locker and walked around the airport. Anya and Julia couldn't leave the secure area, because they were Ukrainian, so we all stayed with them. After eating, walking, and refreshing ourselves in the restrooms, we retrieved our carry-on bags and boarded the plane for Kiev.

Twenty hours after leaving Albuquerque, we filed off the plane at the Borispol airport, just south of Kiev. There were no jet ways; we walked across the tarmac, through a set of double wooden doors, and into the terminal. Our luggage was piled just inside the door -- no moving belts, or even motorized luggage carts. In addition to the allotted luggage for eight people, we had packed two huge extra boxes of antibiotics, painkillers, surgical equipment, books, and teaching supplies. Jude negotiated with the customs officials while Rich, Steve, and Herb Morgan, one of the team who would stay in Kiev, manhandled the boxes. We women gathered all the suitcases and, pushing, pulling and dragging, got in the customs line. The terminal was small and very run down. Its tile floor was grey with grime and several tiles were broken or missing. The walls were drab, dark beige. Water stains on both the acoustical tiles and walls showed the severity of the roof leaks, which apparently no one had made an effort to fix. Finally we got to the head of the line, where several young officials stood in plywood booths with iron bars across the window. We pushed our passports and customs forms under the bars; they asked us a few questions, stamped every piece of paper in sight, and handed us our clearance; and we continued to the doors to the waiting room.

Emerging from the doors Anya and Julia saw their brother. Yaroslav and ran screaming to hug him. With him were a driver and two Kirovograd policemen. Standing nearby were two people to meet the Kiev contingent of the mission team. I looked around and found Lyudmilla's son and his wife. Just before we had left, Lyudmilla had asked me to come over to her house. She gave me most of the money I had paid her for the translation of the documents and a few gifts for her son. I gave the money and gifts to them, and we talked, keeping one eye on the growing stack of luggage on the curb. A white van with two bench seats and open cargo area in the back and a dilapidated, compact car about the size of a compact Toyota were our transportation to Kirovograd. Eleven people and fifteen pieces of luggage had to fit into the two vehicles for the four-hour ride back to Kirovograd.

Yaroslav, the driver, the policemen, Rich, Steve, and Betsy all tried to organize the packing of the van. After several attempts all the luggage was stuffed into the back of the van and the trunk of the car. Rich and Betsy climbed into the van with Yaroslav and the driver while Anya and Julia sat on top of the luggage. I sat in the back seat of the car then Steve and Jude squeezed in on either side of me. The two policemen sat in the front. It was a tight fit. The car could only go about forty-to-fifty kilometers per hour (about thirty miles per hour), making the two-hundred-kilometer trip to Kirovograd seem interminable. Steve and Jude pointed out a few sights that they remembered. As we left the city behind, the landscape grew more like the Great Plains of the Western United States; it reminded me of the stretches I had crossed so many times as a child when we drove from Colorado to visit my grandparents in Kansas.

After about an hour and a half, we pulled over to the side of the road. Anya came jogging back to our car to see if I needed to go to the bathroom. She pointed to the bathroom facilities, some particularly thick areas of the woods alongside the road. The women pushed through the weeds and vines at the edge of the road and wandered into the woods in one direction while the men went another. Then we all squeezed back into the car and van and resumed our journey. An hour later, we made another stop, and while Anya, Julia, Betsy and I again visited the woods, the drivers bought some refreshments at a little roadside restaurant. Most of the way we dozed, although we woke as we passed the vodka factory. The smell of rotting potato and sugar beet pulp was enough to wake us even after our twenty-hour flight.

We tumbled out of the vehicles in Kirovograd into the embrace of a heavily made-up woman with bright red fingernails and a mass of long curly red hair. She was wearing a flowing, flowered dress and carrying armloads of flowers. This was Margarita Nikoliyavna, the principal of School # 11. Even though School # 11 specialized in the instruction of English, Margarita herself spoke no English. We figured out later that she could understand some English, but it probably served her purposes better to avoid letting most people know how much she understood. She handed flowers all around, smothered us in bounteous, perfume-scented hugs, then swept off to another appointment. Anya and Julia ran off immediately to greet their parents, who lived just around the corner from the school, while Yaroslav helped us unload our luggage at the satellite school that would be home to Steve, Jude, and me for the next three weeks. It was a low stucco building with white trim. Once it had been a house, but Margarita had completely gutted it to make the school. Just inside the door an entry foyer led to the office of the teacher and monitor and a classroom. Beyond these two rooms were another classroom and the office of the speech pathologist for the entire school. The speech pathologist's office had a private outside door. A long hallway ran between the bathrooms and exercise room and ended at the dining room. A small kitchen was attached to the dining room. Each room was nicely plastered and painted with polished wood floors. Steve and Jude said it had been full of rubble the previous year because they were in the midst of renovating it.

"How did you like arriving in Kirovograd in a police car?" Yaroslav asked. Until that point I hadn't even realized the run down, old car was a police car. I was much more interested in finding my bed than anything else.

My bedroom was the office of the speech pathologist. Six pieces of a sectional sofa had been pushed together for a bed. On top were with several blankets to even it out. The bed was actually quite comfortable, and when I slept on it, I couldn't tell where the pieces came together. It was like a giant throne. The standard wall unit found in almost every Soviet home and office had been cleared out so I could hang my clothes and put my other things in drawers.

Steve and Jude slept on more traditional fold-down couches in the exercise room, where the students had dance classes and playtime during the school year when they couldn't go outside. There was no wall unit in the exercise room, so they lived out of their suitcases. The cook and caretaker for the school became our cook and caretaker. She had breakfast on the table at 7:00 every morning and stayed until dinner, cooking and cleaning for us. Occasionally her children came, too, but they usually stayed with their grand-parents. That first night, as soon as she had fed us, we washed up as well as we could in the school bathrooms and fell into bed.

Rich and Betsy stayed with Anya, Julia, and Yaroslav's family. Anya's father Oleg Malyuta was a pediatric surgeon who had once served on the Supreme Soviet. He was one of a generation of Soviets who was a little baffled by all the changes that had taken place and very disturbed by the deterioration of the economy and infrastructure. He could no longer support his family or even perform his job properly. The doctors at his children's hospital had to reuse disposable scalpels as many as ten times, and patients had to provide their own drugs and other medical supplies.

Dr. Malyuta's wife Vera had worked at a bank until the bank closed down permanently. Now she worked hard at the state gas company to keep her large family clothed and fed. Ukrainians rarely have three children. It is considered too difficult.

Yaroslav was several years older than his twin sisters. He was in his last year of his doctoral program at the Linguistics University in Kiev and understood idiomatic American English better than anyone else we met in Ukraine. Sometimes we could almost see the wheels turning in his head when he heard a new slang term or an interesting phrase in English. Because of the influence of his industrious parents, Yaroslav was also very much a go-getter, a rarity for those who grew up under Soviet rule.

I was eager to meet Violetta. Rich and Betsy arranged a trip to the orphanage for our first afternoon. Yaroslav drove us and would act as our translator. We turned through the big metal gates in front of the orphanage. The building was H-shaped with the two wings forming a courtyard divided by a landscaped median strip. A few flowers bloomed in the median and a rusty van sat in the drive near the building. Decorative tiles on the outside of the building suggested the care with which it had been built, although a few of them were now missing. Most of the playground equipment was broken and weeds grew in the yard. Except for a few goats the people in the neighborhood kept for milk and meat, no one had done anything about the condition of the landscape. I saw great potential for using the yard as a community garden for the surrounding neighborhood. Perhaps they would start to see the orphanage differently if they came there to garden every day.

Yaroslav led us to the front door but it was blocked. The maintenance man told us to go in a door on the right side of the courtyard. We climbed the precarious concrete steps, entered the door and found ourselves on a landing between flights of stairs. To our left we found the nurse's office, which looked like the nurse's office in my old elementary school. The nurse called the assistant director of the orphanage on the telephone in response to

Yaroslav's inquiries.

It was Sunday and Yaroslav had not called ahead to say we were coming, so Luba, the director, was not at the orphanage. Yaroslav and the assistant director discussed what to do for a while, then they decided that, because Yaroslav had a car, he should go get Luba. He sprinted off leaving us trying to communicate with the assistant director in sign language and doing a lot of smiling at each other. Inside, the orphanage was painted with the same beige and turquoise green paint as every other official building in Ukraine, but it was cleaner than most. The tiles were mostly intact, and everything seemed scrubbed.

We were still standing in front of the nurse's office smiling at the assistant director when Luba arrived. Luba and Yaroslav had talked on the way. When they came in Yaroslav, looked at Luba, she said something briefly, and he told me, "Violetta is no longer here. Her gypsy band came and took her away."

As he said that it was as though a grey fog descended all around me, and the atmosphere became oppressively heavy. As though from a distance, I heard Luba explain and Yaroslav translate that the whole gypsy band had showed up to take Violetta with them. Luba hadn't wanted to let them take her but when the entire gypsy band shows up, she said, "You don't argue with them."

Immediately Luba said that the orphanage had several other children who could be adopted and we could see them. We started on a tour with Luba and assistant director pointing out the children who could be adopted. The experience was more like shopping for a used car than anything else I have ever done. They pointed out their better qualities and made sure I looked them all over carefully. We visited several rooms, making sure I got to look at all the models that were available so I wouldn't miss the best one by accident. I had no idea how to pick the best child for Robert and me. I held a few children, most of whom cried. There was no way I could even think clearly at that point. Rich suggested we come back later.

We started classes on Monday and almost immediately fell into a routine that would vary little over the next three weeks. Despite the fact that I usually like to sleep late I had no trouble getting up early in the morning and reading scripture and preparing for my Bible Study. Then I reviewed the horticulture lesson I would teach that day and sat down to breakfast with Steve, who had also been up early reading the Bible, and Jude, who was just waking up and still trying to find all his clothes. Rich and Betsy generally joined us, and we discussed our English as a Second Language lessons for the day.

Each morning we began the sessions by singing contemporary Christian praise songs with the teachers. Singing is very important in Ukrainian society, and they welcomed the opportunity to learn new songs they could teach their students. It soon became obvious that I could have been better prepared to teach my courses. The teachers didn't know the meaning of the word *hort-iculture*, but most of them, after spending the morning brushing up on American English, would go home or to their *dachas* and try to raise enough food to get them through the winter. My PhD dissertation had been about intensive food production in home gardens to improve nutrition, but I was walking around telling them the American common names of the trees and flowers. When I talked about American houses and home life it sounded too much like bragging about how much we had and they didn't.

The worst days were when I tried out my game, having small groups form businesses and compete against each other. These Ukrainian adults simply could not get it, at least not in the American way. They weren't sticking to their own business, they weren't creating a service or product, and they were helping each other too much. The Soviet system discourages both competitive free enterprise and expressing any imaginative creativity. They refused to try to make a profit off of each other.

On the final day I answered questions about life in America and any other subject they wanted to discuss. Many of the questions were on ways to increase the productivity of their gardens or to how to control insect pests, which is what I should have been talking about in the first place.

In the second session each morning we distributed and discussed the ESL materials. These were classroom resources rather than lessons, but we wanted to make sure they knew all the right answers. My group was made up mostly of teachers from the experimental schools, who already knew a great deal more American English than most of the other teachers. We spent very little time on the ESL resources and more on the Bible Study.

Our American mission team soon learned that there is great variation in the English proficiency of English teachers in Ukraine. The teachers in the Christian schools were quite proficient. They taught in English all day long. The teachers at the regular school # 11 had an adequate grasp of English to teach the subject, although they did not understand all of our American English with our funny accents. We also had a few English teachers from the surrounding schools in smaller towns and villages. For some of them it was difficult even to carry on a conversation in English.

While our students went to work in their vegetable gardens to try to assure survival for the next year, we Americans ate a big lunch, rested a bit, then sat in the sauna and tearoom in the basement of the first experimental school. Margarita had reserved it for our use for as long as we were there. We had long discussions in the lounge there, ranging from philosophy and theology. For our enjoyment Margarita had ordered the best brand of chocolate in the Ukraine. The sauna dressing room was also the only place we could take a hot shower. There was no hot water in Kirovograd in the summer unless it was boiled on the stove. Anya and Julia, who had grown to like hot showers in the United States, often came for a shower, too. After the first few days David, an American missionary who was teaching at the school, began to join us regularly.

My evenings were often long and lonely. One of the Ukrainian teachers frequently came to learn guitar chords for the praise songs from Steve. Jude, Anya, and Julia hung out with other students who had just graduated from high school. Rich and Betsy visited with the Malyutas, and I generally read and listened to music. I felt discouraged about the adoption and disappointed that it had not worked out according to the plans and dreams I had cherished for almost a year. God obviously had different plans.

Back home, Robert had the documents sealed in Santa Fe then sent them to Washington to be taken by courier to the appropriate offices. He had no idea what was happening in Ukraine. We had not yet established a way to contact each other by telephone.

Chapter 7

Let the little children come to me and do not hinder them, for the kingdom of God belongs to such as these. Mark 10:14

One afternoon at the orphanage before naptime was even over, Sveta told Anastasia to get dressed because her Mama had come to see her. Anastasia put on the pretty dress they gave her, and Natasha put a big bow in her hair.

"Why hasn't my Mama ever come to see me before?" she asked.

"This is a new Mama," Natasha told her. "If she likes you, maybe you can go home with her."

Down the hall she went, into the office of the assistant director of the orphanage. A woman smiled at her and held out her arms.

"Go to your Mama," Sveta told her.

"Mama," she said, and climbed on her lap. The woman gave her a hug. This woman was definitely not her Mama, but she would probably be a good Mama. She had a smiley face and was gentle when she touched her. The orphanage women talked about her and another pretty lady said strange words to the Mama. Anastasia sat on the Mama's lap for a while but was very happy when Margarita put some toys on the floor for her to play with. She had just started playing when Julia brought Snijana. Anastasia ran to her and hugged her.

"That's not Mama," whispered Snijana.

"No, but we have to pretend she is so she likes us. She might take us home with her." After a great deal of coaxing Snijana sat on the lady's lap and snuggled against her. Anastasia could see that the woman liked holding

Snijana. Maybe this would work out. She would like to have a Mama. It would be even better if she could have a Papa, too.

The grownups talked about how smart Anastasia was; then Luba asked her to recite her part from "The Wolf and the Kids," which they were practicing for the summer program. She stood up, straightened her pretty dress, winked at Sveta to show that she would do a really good job and recited:

"My kiddies small, my kiddies dear,

Open the door for your Mother is here.

Let me in and I will give you a treat,

For I bring you milk, both rich and sweet."

She bowed and smiled at the Mama. Everyone clapped, so she did a little dance.

Then they asked Snijana to recite her part from "The Fox and the Wolf." She was afraid to. Anastasia finally got Snijana to stand beside her and whispered the part in her ear as she said it, but she didn't say it very loud.

"Come, come, little tree, nice and straight, come to me.

Come, come, little tree, nice and straight, come to me."

They didn't get to stay too long before they were sent back to their room. Pavlik asked what she had been doing.

"A new Mama might want to take me home," she said.

Pavlik looked stricken. "But what about me? Would your Mama take me, too, so we could be brother and sister?"

"I don't know," Anastasia said. "If she really does come back for me, I will ask her."

The woman had seemed nice enough, but Anastasia didn't think much more about her that day. They had an extra practice for the summer program that they would soon present for the patrons. After the summer program, the older kids always left to go to the other orphanage. That would make Anastasia the oldest one in the room. She had been waiting a long time to be the oldest. She already thought of the best things to do, and everyone liked to do what she told them. Being the oldest meant that she would not have to listen to anyone except the grownups. Of course, Pavlik would have to leave with the older kids, because he was going to be five years old. Pavlik had promised that he would check out the new orphanage for her and tell her all the things to look out for when she came. It would be good to have Pavlik there ahead of her, but she would miss him terribly until it was time for her to go to that orphanage.

Chapter 8

Therefore I tell you, do not worry about your life, what you will eat or drink; or about your body, what you will wear. Is not life more important than food, and the body more important than clothes? Matthew 6:25

By the third afternoon in Kirovograd I was thinking more clearly as we met more children. We sat in the assistant director's office drinking tea while several children were brought in. The first was a little girl named Oksana, who cried the whole time she was there. Next came four-year-old Anastasia with a big smile, who rushed up to me and called me Mama. Then they brought in her sister Snijana. Anastasia was so charming and confident as she recited verses I couldn't understand at all, and I loved cuddling Snijana on my lap. This was exactly what I had been looking for. But I had come to adopt one girl, not two. I felt too alone and uncertain to make that decision by myself. Several other children came and went but nothing seemed right. I went back to my room at the school, put a tape of our friend Steve Herrera's music in my walkman and lay on my bed crying in confusion and frustration.

The excitement and anticipation of the past year had shriveled when they told me Violetta was not there and left only blank hopelessness in its place. While I lay there, David came knocking on the door. He didn't go away, even though I ignored his knocks. When I did finally answer the door, he didn't seem to notice my tear-stained face. He made small talk for a little while, then asked me how things were going. I told him how hopeless I felt. He assured me that it would all work out according to God's plan and prayed with me that I would know God's plan in this adoption and would be able to follow it.

Margarita finally had the phone in the school hooked up to receive long distance calls. We could not make calls from the phone, only receive them. We set up a schedule. Steve's wife would call two days a week, and Robert would call on two different days. That way we did not seem so isolated from our families. They would also pass on information to the church about the mission team. Jude's mother called a couple of times, but he was not feeling the separation quite the way us older, married folks were.

On the first day of the second week, as we were coming up the fire escape-like stairs that led to the auditorium where we sang our morning songs Steve said, "There's Lana."

Jude hurried to the top of the stairs and threw his arms around the elegant, long-legged teacher I had not seen before. He turned to me.

"Lana was our interpreter last year."

The team had talked of her constantly of Lana while we were preparing to come, so I knew who she was. Jude introduced us, and Steve told her I was interested in adopting a child from the orphanage. Lana immediately took charge of the adoption, much to Yaroslav's relief. He did not enjoy going to visit the orphanage. My expectations rose from the depths, and I was swimming in hope again because Lana was so optimistic. She arranged a visit to the orphanage that afternoon.

Visiting the orphanage with Lana was a totally different experience. She told me about each child and asked pertinent questions of the caregivers and administrators. I selected one of the younger girls and asked if I could adopt her. We went back to Luba's office and looked up the information on her. Luba said she was not a good risk because of her mother's mental health problems. Of all the children I had seen, Oksana, the one who had cried so much when they brought her into the assistant director's office, was my first choice. Not the perfect match, just the best choice in a difficult situation. Luba gave us all the information on Oksana, and I wrote a new application saying we wanted to adopt her.

The next day Lana took me to visit the regional Center for Adoptions. This was in the basement of the Regional office building in downtown Kirovograd. We walked into the office, but everyone kept working. When someone finally looked up, Lana told them what we wanted. The woman told us to wait in the hall. The bordered tile floor, the varnished wooden chairs, the green paint halfway up the walls with beige above -- it was like sitting in the hall waiting to be called into the principal's office. Sometime later a secretary came and told us that the Inspector could see us now. We went into the office and stood in front of her desk as she took the papers and looked them over. She frowned at us suspiciously.

"How did you know what papers to bring?" she asked.

Lana interpreted, and I explained how Anya had called Kiev and talked with the Ministry of Education.

She took the papers but did not make any promises.

Next we went to the City Orphanage Inspector's office. The office was much more open with no dark hallway waiting area. They invited us to sit in front of an empty desk. The director was not in, but the three people who worked there were very interested in America and spent more than an hour asking me questions about the United States, my motivation for adopting, and my life in general. When the director came, he had even more questions for us. He knew a little English and was eager to practice, so he asked questions in English. I did not understand all of his questions. It had been a long time since he had practiced his English. Everyone in the office was very pleased that we had come to see them and impressed that we had so many official looking papers, but did not make any promises about helping us with the adoption.

Yuri, a teacher at School #11, was the son of a well-known lawyer in town. In the middle of our second week of teaching Yuri returned from a year in the United States. Lana and I spent an afternoon talking with him, and he agreed to see if his mother could help us in any way.

At the end of our second week, the school arranged a picnic for the teachers and us. The teachers had not been paid in several months. Because we didn't want them to use either their limited supply of money or their food reserves for winter, we offered to provide all the food for a typical American picnic. Steve and I went shopping with Mrs. Malyuta to buy the supplies. Yaroslav drove us to the market and sat in the car to keep it from being stolen while we shopped.

Although the official Ukrainian economy was the worst in the world, the underground economy flourished. At the edge of the market men sat on the ground selling parts from their broken down cars or various items they had cleaned out of their garages. Behind them in long, crowded rows with narrow aisles, vendors sold clothing, toys, dishes and plastic-ware, cleaning supplies, diapers, oriental rugs, and anything else they could buy wholesale and sell retail. Piles of locally grown organic fruits and vegetables, imported oranges and bananas, cookies and crackers, and all kinds of prepared foods abounded. The market was teeming with customers. Gypsies lured people to have their fortunes told or buy their wares, and housewives exchanged gossip as they bought their food for the day. There was almost a carnival atmosphere about the market. We pushed our way to the money exchange kiosk, and got in line to exchange our money.

Inflation was down to around forty percent from a high of ten thousand percent in 1993. Most Ukrainians either bought things with their money as soon as they got it or changed it into American dollars. Few people were paid consistently in their regular jobs, and salaries were the equivalent of forty to one hundred American dollars per month. Prices were about half what we would pay at home. As a result almost everyone participated in the underground economy. The government had stopped printing money and was printing coupons, whose value changed daily, as a stopgap measure. Coupons functioned like money but were not considered real money by the government, which I suppose reduced their responsibility for a coupon's value. American one hundred dollar bills had become the standard of trade. The bills had to be new, crisp, and unmarked in any way. While we were there the exchange rate fluctuated around 184,000 Ukrainian coupons to the dollar.

As we stood in line at the kiosk the woman in front of Mrs. Malyuta offered to exchange her coupons with us for a slightly higher rate than the booth was offering. We agreed because we would both benefit. The fist full of coupons she gave us filled my purse. We exchanged a second one hundred dollar bill at the booth, asking for ten thousand and twenty thousand coupon bills in case vendors didn't have the right change. As Mrs. Malyuta counted the money and passed it to me, I stuffed my pockets full of money and crammed a few more bills in my purse. When I couldn't carry any more, I passed it to Steve, who stuffed his pockets full, then loaded it into one of the plastic bags we had brought along to carry our purchases.

When we had all the money more or less concealed, I pulled out the list Anya had made in both Ukrainian and English. The first item was twenty pounds of meat. Steve and I followed Mrs. Malyuta as she plowed through the crowd and into the big, beige building in the center of the market. It was alive with the buzz of bargaining voices and flies. The sweet and spicy scents of the flower and honey booths met us at the entrance. But before we even got past the first booths, we were hit by the smell of blood and fish and fresh meat from the meat market at the center of the building.

We could have bought a whole fish, chicken or goose, a freshly severed hog's head, or any number of other unidentified cuts of meat that lay unwrapped on the tables. If someone wanted a two-pound piece of the side of beef or pork that was hanging in the booth, the butcher just chopped it off. But we were looking for twenty pounds of lamb for *shashliki*. More than halfway through the market we found the right booth. As Mrs. Malyuta bargained for what we needed, the proprietor's of other booths eyed us and called out to convince her that their meat was better, or cheaper, and that she should buy from them. When she had made the deal, the butcher wrapped the meat in paper and dropped it into one of the plastic bags Steve carried while I paid for it.

Next we needed twenty pounds of potatoes. We went outside to the hundreds of other plywood and canvas booths that surrounded the main market building. The section where vegetables were sold was not far from the entrance to the building. We examined the potatoes available from several booths. Mrs. Malyuta and I agreed on the best looking potatoes and she bargained for them. With lots of head shaking and forceful argument they

struck a deal; the vendor added up the amount on her calculator and showed it to me. Steve and I examined the bills until we found the right amount
and paid for the potatoes, then dumped them from the scale into another
bag.

We tramped onward, buying onions, carrots, cabbage, cucumbers, and
the other things we would need. Although Mrs. Malyuta did not speak
English, it was easy to shop together. I showed her the next thing on the list,
and she took us to the right booth. We examined the produce, picked out the
best, comparing what each of us had selected, then handed them to the
vendor. The vendor weighed them, added up the purchase on their cal-
culators, and showed me the amount, Steve and I fumbling around until we
found the right bills to pay for the produce. Then the vendor dropped the
purchase into one of Steve's plastic bags. Each time, vendors in the surrounding booths, who were selling the same things, would give us mal-
evolent looks because we were not buying from them

As the bags filled, the strings began to cut into Steve's fingers. His arms
were aching as we marched from stall to stall. But we continued around the
open-air market, choosing the best of everything they had. Each purchase
was made from a different vendor. I carried milk, mayonnaise, and sour
cream in unlabeled glass jars. Mrs. Malyuta safeguarded the eggs, which we
bought last. They didn't come in a carton. She piled them into a plastic bag
and carried it through the crowds, very carefully. Finally, we shouldered our
way back to where Yaroslav was waiting in the car. Yaroslav extracted the
strings from Steve's hands, put the bags in the trunk (except for the eggs,
which Mrs. Malyuta held on her lap), and drove us home.

That afternoon we worked in the main school kitchen, across the street from the classroom building, to prepare American-style potato salad and coleslaw, deviled eggs, and sliced cucumbers and tomatoes. As we climbed the back stairs to the kitchen, a rat peeked at us from under the back steps, but the kitchen cat wandered through several times while we were working so the rat didn't bother us. We found big pots to boil eggs and potatoes. We sliced cabbage, tomatoes, and cucumbers on the big chopping block in the middle of the room and mixed and stirred in the big bowls from the kitchen; then we washed everything and left the kitchen cleaner than we had found it. That really wasn't very hard to do.

After we had finished preparing the American dishes, we went to the Malyuta's where Mrs. Malyuta showed us how to make *shashliki*. It is Ukrainian *shish-kabob* and a favorite at picnics. *Shashliki* involved cutting a lot of onions (which Jude got to do by virtue of his junior status on the team), mixing large quantities of marinade, and cutting up the twenty pounds of meat we had bought. While the *shashliki* marinated, Mrs. Malyuta fed us all as we watched a Bill Cosby video Yaroslav used in his classes.

Saturday morning, as we were boarding the bus to go to the lake for the picnic, the teacher Yuri told me that Oksana was not available for adoption because her mother had not relinquished her, even though she was in the orphanage. I was getting desperate. By now over half our time in Ukraine was over, and I had gotten nowhere on the adoption.

We rode the ancient bus several miles between rolling fields of wheat and sunflowers, lined with hedgerows. Again I was struck with the similarity with America. I could almost believe I was going to the Kansas farm I had inherited from my Dad. The final stretch of road was through a little wood; then the road opened onto a lake. The driver turned, drove along the lake, and parked near the shelter that had been reserved for our picnic.

Even though we had explained very clearly in all the classes that we would be supplying the food for an American-style picnic, all the teachers had brought something. Several teachers made *vareniki*, a kind of national dish in Ukraine. I had grown up eating *vareniki* but always considered it a Russian dish because my grandmother often prepared it for us. It is a kind of large, triangular shaped dumpling made by wrapping noodle dough around several kinds of fillings. My grandmother most often used potatoes, dry cottage cheese, or apples. In early summer in Ukraine they used mostly curds or cherries. One of the teachers had caught a large fish that was grilled over the fire with the *sashliki*. None of the teachers ate the coleslaw or potato salad because it had mayonnaise in it, and they were afraid it would make them sick. We threw out the coleslaw but had potato salad for lunch every day for the rest of our stay in Ukraine. None of us got sick.

Near the shelter was a dock from which we could swim, and a quarter of the way around the lake was a diving tower and paddleboat dock. We stripped off the clothes we had worn over our swimsuits and jumped in. The water was a little muddy but was warm and fun to swim in. After less than an hour of swimming, we noticed that the water had stripped the color from Betsy's hair. One of the teacher's offered to help her get more color because none of the Ukrainian women will let their hair show grey. They were appalled that Betsy was willing to let it remain grey until she went home. My skin becan to burn after one more dip, so I abandoned swimming for the rest of the day. Betsy and I speculated that it must have had a very strong dose of industrial pollutants in it. Some of the people were able to stay in the water most of the afternoon though.

After I had eaten, I started walking the paths around the lake, pondering what I would do. I knew the answer was right in front of my face, but I couldn't see it. Lana joined me and told me that sometimes she gets pictures in her head that tell her what to do. She had gotten a picture in her head that told her we should adopt Anastasia and Snijana. Shortly before we left the lake Betsy joined me to walk up the entrance road and told me that she thought Anastasia and Snijana were the perfect children for us. I agreed with them but had resisted saying so because of the added trouble and expense of adopting two children.

That night, in my dreams, the girls I had seen so often kneeling at the rail in the church turned around, and they were Anastasia and Snijana. It felt so right that I wondered why I had wasted so much time going down other paths. Now I could see where God had been leading me for the past eight years.

Chapter 9

Why, you do not even know what will happen tomorrow. What is your life? You are a mist that appears for a while, then vanishes. Instead you ought to say, "If it is the Lord's will we will live and do this or that." James 4:14 – 15

Early the next morning, Jude and I went to the post office to make a call to Robert. We crossed the entry lobby and entered a large room with glass-doored cubicles around three sides. It was one of the most pleasant public buildings I had seen in Ukraine so far. Diffused light came in from the big, whitewashed storefront windows along the front. In the center were wooden seats. It could very well have been a Depression-Era waiting room in any American city. The telephone booths each contained an old-fashioned black telephone and a little stool. Whole families were crowded into some booths that Sunday morning, talking with loved ones in another country.

Jude went to the desk at one end of the room. He wrote down Robert's name and number on the little slip of paper and handed it to the woman at the desk. There were so many people waiting that they said we could only talk for four minutes. We paid for four minutes to America; she gave us a receipt, and told us to go to booth number eight. I was to sit in the booth and wait until the phone rang. After several minutes the phone rang, and I quickly picked it up expecting to talk with Robert.

"Hello," I said.

"This is the operator. Please hold for your party," a heavily accented voice said.

I waited a few minutes more, clutching the phone to my ear, until the operator had made the connection and Robert was on the other end. The line was filled with static and kept cutting out. There was also a noticeable time delay, so that we would both start talking at the same time when we didn't think the other person was saying anything. I finally managed to comm.unicate to him that Violetta was gone and that there were two girls available I liked. "Can we adopt both of them?" I asked.

Robert said "We've taken in three foster children at a time before, how difficult could two little girls be?"

I hadn't told him half of what I wanted to say or asked half of what I wanted to ask when the operator cut in and said, "thirty seconds left."

"I love you," I said. "I will do everything I can to get the girls."

"I love you, too. I wish I were there with you."

And the line went dead.

After talking with Robert, I felt even more alone and overwhelmed, but more certain that we should proceed with the adoption of Anastasia and Snijana.

Back at School #11 Betsy's class was on teaching methods, Rich and Steve taught a combined class on history and business, Jude taught American cinema, and I taught horticulture. There were four classes, but only three weeks. In the last week of classes, the students who would have been in my horticulture class wanted to go to Jude's American cinema class. Since I was free for the first two hours each morning, Lana and I made the rounds of the adoption offices.

The city adoption authorities said the regional authorities had to start the process. The regional authorities said the national authorities had to approve it first. The national authorities, when we called them, said that the city authorities had to approve it first. I had no idea what to do next. Fortunately Lana did. She arranged a meeting with Margarita, who had more political clout than Lana. Margarita took me under her wing. I went to teach my Bible Study while Margarita made phone calls.

Margarita had given us the key to the private lounge next to her office, where we met after class to drink tea or coffee and discuss the day's classes. It had just been repaired and carpeted, although it was very sparsely furnished. There were shelves along one wall and a small grouping of modern furniture in the opposite corner. One day, Jude and I finished class early and came into the lounge to find Margarita signing some papers with a man and a woman. They were tenants of a house Margarita had recently bought for an experimental school. Margarita evicted them, and they were there to complete the agreement and celebrate the fact that Margarita had found them somewhere else to live. They invited us to toast the eviction with them. We hung back, but Margarita was very insistent. Not wanting to offend her, we sat.

The man filled glasses with champagne for the ladies and then poured vodka for Jude and himself. Jude got half a shot glass in honor of his age. Margarita made a speech about the wonderful agreement they had reached and we drank our drinks. The glasses refilled, the man made a speech about how wonderful Margarita was for finding them an even better place to live, and we drank again. Then the woman said something and we drained our glasses again. They toasted Jude's ability to speak Russian, which was rapidly becoming less inhibited, if also less accurate. The man was from Russia. Margarita told them that I was going to adopt some girls and that she was going to help me. She also told them my grandparents came from Russia. For that the man said I should drink a shot of vodka. By now he had downed at least four shots and was unrelenting. He promised me that if I would drink one shot he would leave me alone. Jude and I talked him down to half a shot. He said something about us being comrades and fellow countrymen, I closed my eyes, held my breath and downed the vodka. That was the only vodka I drank in all my time in Ukraine, but coming after two glasses of champagne, it had quite a jolt. We talked some more about how wonderful Margarita was, what we were doing in Ukraine, and their new place to live. We ate some chocolates, drank a final toast to their new home, and said good-bye.

By the time everyone else showed up for lunch, the toasting was over and Jude and I were a bit tipsy, but Margarita had committed in front of other people that she was going to help me adopt some girls. Now she had to produce results. She made calls all over the city with renewed enthusiasm. Finally, she got the district judge to agree to a hearing the Tuesday after the end of classes.

I called Robert immediately. He arranged to leave the United States Friday evening to be in Ukraine for the hearing. He would bring the signed and sealed paperwork needed to complete the adoption. We were elated to have scheduled the hearing so quickly and expected to be taking the girls home within two to three weeks. Robert had contacted the embassy in Warsaw, where we would have to get the girl's U.S. entry visas approved, and they were prepared for us.

Behind the scenes, there was some scrambling to decide what to do with me after Steve and Jude left. Rich and Betsy would be touring Ukraine with the Malyutas. I couldn't continue living in the school, and the price the one good hotel in town charged for foreigners was way too high. Lana solved the problem by inviting me to stay with her family. I accepted immediately. Even though I was barely aware of it in my concern about the adoption, God was providing for my every need.

Because there were no flights out of Ukraine on weekends, Steve and Jude had to leave on Thursday. They would spend the night in Kiev with the team members there, then fly out on Friday. I helped them load their things into the car that would take them to Kiev, then brought my suitcase out. Lana arrived with a driver to take me to her house.

Lana, her husband and daughter lived with her parents around the corner from the orphanage. The house, like others nearby, was built right on the sidewalk with a wide gate going into the yard on one side. As we turned into the driveway, Lana hopped out to open the green painted metal gate. She showed me the plaque, attached below the elaborate brickwork on the corner of the house that stated it was the best-maintained house in the area.

Behind the green gate a short driveway led to the garage. Attached to the garage was a summer kitchen, filled with Lana's furniture. They used a smaller kitchen at the back of this building for cooking. Lana led me across a paved patio and up the back porch steps into their house. Just inside was a little entry foyer between the winter kitchen and a storeroom. Two doors opened off the foyer, one leading to the two rooms the five of them would share, and the other leading to the two rooms Robert and I would share. Lana told me our half of the house had been her grandmother's, and the other half her parents' part.

My first night there was the one-year anniversary of Lana's

grandmother's death. In Ukraine, on the one-year anniversary of a death, it is traditional to invite all the neighbors to a memorial dinner. Long tables in the paved yard between the house and summer kitchen were set with their best tablecloths and all the plates and glasses the family owned. Chairs and benches crowded the sides of the table. A picture of Lana's grandmother, draped with an embroidered prayer cloth, was placed on a small table on the back porch. It was a real privilege to be part of so important an evening and an opportunity to better understand the closeness of families in this culture.

As guests arrived, Lana and I carried heaping plates of sliced vegetables, potato salad (to which the mayonnaise had been added at the last minute), layered salads of beets, cabbage, carrots and other vegetables, plates of stewed rabbit, jellied meat, sausage sandwiches and loaf after loaf of bread to the table. A big pot of fruit compote, made by boiling and straining fruit in water, adding sugar and straining the mixture, stood in the kitchen. We poured glasses of this for all the women and children. Lana's husband and father served vodka to all the men. As plates were emptied, her mother supplied more food to be served. When guests left, more took their place. Lana and I removed their plates and took them to her sister to be washed and ready for the next guests. All the guests ate seated at the tables, rather than standing around or perched on the edges of chairs with plates in their laps, as they would have in the United States. Everyone politely looked the other way when the ninety-four-year-old woman who lived behind Lana's parents loaded up her purse with enough food to last her for the next few days. Many of the guests thought I was an out-of-town relative as I helped serve the meal. When all the guests had been served, Lana told me to sit and served me, and finally the family ate and Lana's sister and mother cleaned up.

Tension was apparent that night between Lana and her older sister. Lana laughed and visited with the guests, serving the food her sister and mother had spent most of the day preparing, while her sister spent much of the evening in the back kitchen washing dishes and preparing more food to serve. Lana's sister is a professional cook. Lana is a good cook, but her greatest talent lies in more academic and unconventional directions. Her sister seem-ed to feel safer sticking with conservative tradition and was a little wary of Lana's involvement with Americans. She avoided contact with me the entire time I was there.

The next morning, Lana and I walked downtown to submit some papers to the people at the Center for Adoptions, then to the school. We arrived just as Rich and Betsy were making a presentation of some money and other gifts to the school. I stood with them and Margarita and had my picture taken, then was led away by some of my Bible study students to a tea they had prepared for me. They heated the water in a beautiful silver *samovar* and made the tea in a hand painted china teapot. We sat and talked of life in Ukraine and their appreciation that I had come so far to help them teach their students. They presented me with a beautiful embroidered towel made by one of the teachers.

We were still drinking tea when Lana came in and said we needed to take more papers downtown. I rushed out and went downtown with Lana. I felt a little awkward about being rude and not staying long at the tea, but the adoption was the first thing on my mind, and I didn't want anything to interfere with its successful completion.

Living with Lana, I learned how she differed from most Ukrainians I met. She said she had always thought differently from everyone around her.

She identified with different characters in the stories she had read when she was in elementary school. While she was working on a master's degree in education she had wanted to do research on the way children learn, but the professors would not let her do anything that might show that the traditional Soviet way of rote learning, memorization, and stifling of independent thinking was wrong.

Lana was trying to put together a charitable organization of Christian women in Ukraine who would raise funds for the orphanage. These funds would not just be given to the orphanage, they would be used to hire people to do the work that was needed in the orphanage and pay those people. In that way both the orphanage and the community would benefit and more people might begin to see that these children could be an asset to the community rather than a drain on resources. The general attitude was that the orphaned and abandoned children were from the bottom level of society, because their parents had been. Many of the parents had suffered some form of mental illness, and many Ukrainians believed that any form of mental illness could be inherited. Among Ukrainians who attended the Orthodox church the belief that the sins of the fathers would be visited on the children dominated their beliefs, with very little understanding that God forgives and forgets.

Lana was still in her early thirty's but she had held three different jobs in her working life. All of them had been teaching jobs, but her lack of desire to find a position and stick with it for a lifetime upset her mother. Lana had ideas she would never be able to carry out in Ukrainian society, but she loved Ukraine and never wanted to leave it. By the time we left Ukraine I considered Lana one of my best friends in the world, and she remains so to this day.

Sergei, Lana's husband, had figured out how to manage a business in the free enterprise system, atypical among Ukrainians. He was Vice President of the Mercedes dealership and a large auto repair shop. On Friday we visited the business. On the outside it looked like an American car dealership, except that there weren't any cars on the lot. There was one car in the showroom, which was small by American standards. Around the back the repair shop was a huge, cavernous building with several stalls. Through some carved wooden doors off the showroom was a pool room and bar for the more influential or wealthy clients. More people sat in offices than you would expect for a business this size. I'm not sure what all of them did and I'm not sure they did either. There was one man who sent and received faxes. I think he was also capable of translating faxes into or from German or English if the need arose. Sergei's upstairs office could only be called shabby luxury. The carved doors, Oriental carpets, wood paneling, and big wooden desk, were all a little worn and dusty.

Although the place didn't look too foreign to my American eyes, business practices were quite different. Ukrainian thinking is a mixture of European, Soviet, and Oriental attitudes and the business practices are a reflection of that thinking. Businessmen never come right out and say what they want; yet doing business there isn't nearly as difficult as in the Far East. Much drinking and socializing goes along with doing business, but in the end, hard bargaining is what gets the deal made. Sergei seemed quite good at all of that, although sometimes the drinking took its toll. He lost his inhibitions too quickly to be really good at the hard bargaining.

Saturday morning Lana went to the market. I expected to go to the orphanage to play with the girls when she returned. But when she re-appeared, she looked distressed and said she had to go downtown right away. I relaxed in the back yard while she was gone, sitting on a chaise lounge, eating yellow cherries off the tree that hung over their house, reading a book, and playing with their Russian blue cat Suzanna. After about two hours Lana bolted back through the gate.

"Parliament passed a new constitution last night. The President wouldn't let them go home until they did," she announced.

"What does that mean?" I asked.

"It means that we finally have a government," she said. "But it also means that all the laws are thrown out. Nothing legal can be done until new laws are passed."

"You mean we can't have our adoption hearing on Tuesday? They can't just throw out all the laws, can they?"

"They did. We cannot do anything about the adoption until new laws are passed. The adoption laws will probably not be the first ones passed, either, because other laws are more urgent."

"But they can't do that to us," I protested.

I flashed back to when I was teaching a University class about vegetable production. One of the students came into class late and announced that the Challenger had blown up. I said, very matter of factly "No. That did not happen." It was unthinkable. For a moment the grey fog descended again; then I started arguing with Lana that it really hadn't happened, that it couldn't have happened. I was dumbfounded that everything in the country could come to a total standstill while the laws were rewritten.

"This is the first Constitution we have had since the fall of communism.

It is very good to have a constitution. Anarchy is not good." Lana said, as though I was a little dense and I couldn't understand that. But I wanted to adopt the girls. Why did they have to pass a constitution just when I had almost succeeded?

We went to the orphanage where I played with the girls while Lana talked with Luba about what might be done to complete the adoption. Neither Lana nor I was ready to give up. On the way back from the orphanage a voice in my head said, "You aren't going to get these girls until you get your financial situation in order." Robert and I tended to buy things when we wanted to and be too optimistic about when the money would come in to pay for them. Since both of us were self-employed, we should have been more conservative in our projections. I knew Robert and I had to find a way to eliminate our credit card debt and be more responsible with our purchases. It was suddenly quite clear that our finances and this adoption were intimately related.

Lana's daughter Anna had been staying with Sergei's parents in his hometown for two weeks. That evening we went to pick her up. We drove for almost an hour along the highway before we turned off onto a dirt road. The road was a little muddy, and it got narrower and muddier the farther we drove. After a few miles, we were driving along a narrow, mud track between rolling yellow wheat fields. Water puddled in every low spot. Each time we drove through a mud puddle Lana would tell Sergei she thought we would get stuck and each time Sergei gunned the Mercedes through. Finally, in the middle of one particularly large puddle the Mercedes ground to a halt. Sergei rocked the car back and forth. We just dug deeper and deeper into the mud. As the tires spun in the mud, Lana and I discussed whether we would need to get out and push. We finally decided that we should. Just as we got our shoes off, so we would not ruin them, the tires dug down to solid ground and the car rocketed out of the mud.

As we climbed the next hill, Lana pointed toward the sun, low in the sky, and I saw a charming, little village nestled in the hills near a lake. It had a peacefulness about it that was not present in the cities of Ukraine. We drove almost to the center of the village, where we pulled into a yard. Sergei's father came out of the run-down little house to show us around. He was staying there during the summer growing vegetables in a large garden. Behind the house was a traditional thatched roof hut with a dirt floor. As Sergei and his father visited, Lana and I picked raspberries from the patch behind the house and looked at the big melon patch his father had planted but none of the melons were ripe yet.

From the village we went into the town where Anna was staying with her grandmother, her aunt and two cousins. We had already eaten dinner, but they immediately began preparing fresh vegetables and cheese, butter and sour cream, and some very good homemade sausage. While Lana, her mother-in-law and sister-in-law were preparing the meal Anna showed me the cow, the pig and the other animals she had helped care for during her visit. We ate outside under a little wooden shelter. Since I couldn't talk with anyone except Lana and Anna, and I was already full from my earlier meal, I just ate lots of cucumbers and smiled at everyone. Before we left, they gave us some vegetables and a couple of gallons of milk from their cows. Anna fell asleep on my lap on the way home. She had spent much of her time for the past two weeks leading the cow along the side of the road to graze. She had been up early, gone to bed late, and was very tired. I was pleased to be able to see more of Ukraine and learn how people live, so I could tell the girls when we were able to bring them home.

Lana searched for someone to take me to Borispol to meet Robert on Sunday. A driver she knew offered to make the trip for fifty dollars, but Lana wanted to find someone who had to go to Kiev anyway and would not charge. She finally found Mikhail, a local man who had business to conduct in Kiev. She arranged for him to come for me at around 6:00 a.m. Sunday morning. Lana gave me some bread, cheese, sausage, cherries, and cucumbers to take; then we sat waiting for Mikhail. Every few minutes we went out to the road to look, but there was no sign of him. He finally arrived around 8:00 a.m. Lana lectured him for some time, made him promise he would take good care of me, and told me to get into the back seat. We drove around Kirovograd for a while looking for someone else. Mikhail spoke a little English and tried to explain to me what he was doing, but I wasn't too sure. We dropped off one person who was riding with us, switched drivers and were on our way. The new Mercedes sometimes traveled at 100 km/hr (60 mph), which seemed terribly fast and reckless on Ukrainian roads. We made the trip in three hours. Mikhail had me at the airport a little after one. He walked me to the door, explaining that he would return at about four o'clock, and left. I had not been left alone in Ukraine before now, but felt comfortable enough in the small airport terminal.

The terminal was a little cleaner than the customs area had been. My experiences in most of Ukraine left me feeling like I had been transported back to about 1934. The airport terminal was solidly in the sixties. There were turquoise and white plastic seats, little candy-selling booths set into the concrete walls, big automatic sliding glass doors at the entrance, and what was probably asbestos tile on the floor.

Robert's plane was not scheduled to arrive until 2:30 p.m., so I bought a Coke at a little vending booth and settled down on the hard plastic seat to wait. The terminal smelled a little of mildew and a little of unwashed bodies jammed together. I periodically went outside to sit on the low concrete wall for a breath of fresh air. Then I returned to the terminal to check the clock. When a crowd started to gather at the door from the customs area, I joined them. People were emerging one and two at a time from the door and the crowd pressed as closely as possible around it. Finally I saw Robert. I shoved toward the front of the crowd, calling his name. He spotted me and met me halfway through the crowd. I hugged him, kissed him and told him that we would have to wait a while for our ride. We bought a couple more Cokes and sat down on the hard seats, where I explained that a new constitution had been passed while he was en route and we couldn't get anyone to do anything now. He was deflated and angry at the news. We completely forgot about asking for God's help and spent the next few hours pondering ways we might be able to change reality or get someone to let us adopt using the old laws so we could take the girls home immediately. At 4:00 we went outside to wait. Mikhail didn't come. A friendly taxi driver did come and talk to us in an attempt to practice his English and get a fat fare from American customers.

By 6:00 p.m. Mikhail still hadn't come. Robert couldn't understand why Lana hadn't hired the driver for fifty dollars. He would have stayed with us, and we could have driven back to Kirovograd in the light and seen the landscape. With the help of the friendly taxi driver, I went to the airport phone room, a bare concrete room with phones on folding tables rather than in little booths. I called Lana and asked if she knew anything about where Mikhail might be. She said that she would try to find out and that I should call her back in about an hour. An hour later, without the friendly taxi driver and without the right change, I tried to call back. I finally got the operator to understand what I wanted, and she dialed the number. Lana had been waiting for my call. She said Mikhail's father didn't know where he was and we should keep waiting. We went back outside to wait. The friendly taxi driver returned and offered to take us to Kirovograd for $250. We bought more Cokes and waited some more. The friendly taxi driver stayed with us and agreed that he would take us for $200. We still refused. He finally lowered his price to $150.

At 9:00 p.m. the airport was nearly abandoned. One by one, banks of lights went out. They shooed us outside to sit on the concrete wall. We decided it was time to find the friendly taxi driver. I found him and we were heading back toward Robert and the luggage, when Mikhail came striding across the empty parking lot. He explained that he had some trouble with his business, which Lana later told us was Mafia business. We piled into the Mercedes and took off. The return trip took only four hours even though it was night and visibility was often poor. At one point we came to the end of some new construction, marked only by a pile of gravel, which we plowed into. We backed out, found the connection with the old highway and sped on. Robert slept most of the way after his twenty-hour flight, but I was wired on caffeine and nerves and stayed awake the whole way. I kept trying to talk with Robert but got nothing back except hard to comprehend grunts.

We finally made it to Lana's house at 1:00 a.m. Lana stood just inside the gate in her bathrobe holding a loaf of bread with a little dish of salt on top of it.

"What's that for?" Robert asked.

"It is a tradition dating from Roman times," Lana replied. "Bread and salt to welcome guests."

Robert was fascinated to be participating in so ancient a tradition, although we did not stay up to eat any of the bread. We went right to bed and slept late the next morning.

The next morning, I showed Robert around the little yard, which felt like home to me by now. An outdoor pit latrine on one side of the summer kitchen was their only toilet. There was a sauna on that side of the yard and a solar shower on the other side. Behind the shower Lana's father kept rabbits and behind the summer kitchen he grew a small garden. Then the chicken coop sat behind the garden. Robert felt right at home. He had grown up on a dairy from where they milked by hand and his father farmed with horses until he was about four years old.

Over the next two days we visited all the officials in Kirovograd again but were told in no uncertain terms that nothing could be done right now. They told us it wouldn't be long before the new laws were passed. We kept pressuring but finally ran out of people to talk to and arguments to make. Margarita even called the representative of the President in Kirovograd. She did not have enough information about us and the girls when she called, and he had just laughed at her. She was angry, embarrassed, and discouraged, as well as very sad that we could not get the girls. We resolved to come back as soon as the new laws were passed.

That left five more days in Kirovograd as tourists. The first day we walked with Lana to School # 11. One of the teachers met us there. She unlocked a door and took us into one of the larger rooms in the school, filled with World War II mementos.

"The war came through Kirovograd twice, once as the Germans advanced and again as the Russians pushed them back," she told us. "The holes in the buildings across the street were made by the German mortars." She referred to the rat-infested kitchen we had cooked in earlier. "This is my uniform and some pictures of me with some other resistance fighters."

"You were in the war?" Robert asked.

"Yes, I was an underground resistance fighter when they came through the first time, then I was a radio operator for the Russian army. I was very young at the time. Outside we have a rose garden with a rose planted for each of the school alumni who were lost in the war."

We walked outside and looked at the rose garden. Although my Dad had been an artillery officer in the Pacific during the war, and I had heard a few of his stories, being in a place where it actually happened made it much more real.

On the way home, Lana showed us a statue of Lenin that stood in one of the parks.

"They have talked about taking it down a number of times, but nobody knows where the pigeons might roost if they take it down, so they leave it up for the pigeons," she said.

The ancient Scythians were known for the strong and masterful metal work they provided the Romans and for vast hoards of gold. They roamed the steppes north of the Black Sea and mined their gold from the hills in what is now called Kirovograd Region. The first Russian Empire had its capital in Kiev and its southern outpost at Elizavetsgrad, which later became

Kirovograd. The earthen embankments that protected the empire still stand around the old part of the city.

In later years Cossacks roamed the area, and some of the great Cossack Hetmen were local boys. With the development of agriculture and long distance transportation, Ukraine became the breadbasket of Europe. Poland and Russia fought over and divided Ukraine between them. During most of its history Ukraine was not an independent nation, but the people held onto their identity as Ukrainians. Stalin did his best to kill off the fiercely independent Cossack spirit by creating an artificial famine and importing hundreds of Russians to replace the thousands of Ukrainians who starved, but people like Lana still clung to their Ukrainian culture.

Just outside the ancient earthen embankments, Lana took us down a little gravel path. We emerged in a little meadow that looked like someone had just mowed it with a scythe. Lanky Siberian elms surrounded the little clearing and was very hushed, but also unsettling, for reasons we did not initially understand. In the center stood a sort of obelisk, set up recently by Ukrainian standards. As we stood beneath the trees, Lana told us about the Jewish community of Ukraine. The founder of Hasidic Judaism was born in Ukraine, and Ukraine still has the fourth largest Jewish community in the world. In 1939, some cities in Ukraine were fifty percent Jewish. Kirovograd did not have that large a percentage of Jews, but there were several living there. Most were murdered by the Nazis and buried in mass graves. One of those graves was beneath our feet. The light filtering through the trees and the silence, even in the middle of the city, heightened our awareness of the sacredness of the place.

As we walked, Lana told us Ukrainian legends and folk tales. One of the most charming was a story about the creation of Ukraine. When God was creating different countries, He asked various people what they wanted. The Russians wanted the biggest land so God made their land stretch from Europe to the Pacific ocean. The Swiss said, "Give us the biggest mountains," so God gave them the Alps. The Germans said, "Give us the most trees," so God gave them the Black Forest. The Norwegians said, "Give us the best seaports," so God gave them the fiords. The Kenyans said, "Give us the most animals," so God gave them the Serengetti. Finally God asked the Ukrainians what they wanted, and they said they just wanted whatever was left. For their humility God dumped out what was left in his bag: the richest earth, the most beautiful mountains, the greenest forests in all the world. "That is a legend that dates back to Roman times," she said with a twinkle in her eye. Just about everything she told us about was supposed to date back to Roman times.

Chapter 10

"For I know the plans I have for you," said the Lord. "Plans to prosper you and not to harm you, plans to give you hope and a future." Jeremiah 29:11

Anastasia waited impatiently but quietly for naptime to be over. Two days earlier her new Papa came to see her. A Papa! All her life Anastasia had dreamed of having a Papa. One thing about Mama and Papa was funny though. They never talked directly to her but always had Lana tell her things. She still loved to play with them. She spent the long naptime trying to think of ways to make them laugh. They seemed to laugh and smile more than other adults she had known.

When Sveta said they could get up from their nap, she dressed hurriedly and went to wait by the door. She kept peeking around it to see if anyone was in the cloakroom. Before long Luba came and took her to the office where her new parents waited with Snijana and Lana.

"Today you are going to go for a visit with your new parents," said Luba.

Lana led them to a car that was waiting in the driveway and introduced them to her husband Sergei and her daughter Anna. To Anastasia and Snijana a ride in a car meant a move to a new orphanage or a trip to the hospital. Anastasia clung nervously to her new Papa. Snijana sat on the lap of her new Mama. She started crying as soon as the car started moving. They drove to a big apartment building. All around the apartment were piles of dirt that the car bumped over.

Lana asked Anastasia and Snijana to stay in the car with Anna, but they did not want to be left behind. They climbed out of the car and clung tightly to Mama and Papa. The apartment building had a big trench around it. Mama carried Snijana across, and Papa swung Anastasia over it then held her hand while they climbed the stairs.

"We bought this flat and are fixing it up," explained Lana "It is on the fourth floor, which is the best floor, and it faces west so we can have some afternoon sun."

Sergei led the way up the bare concrete steps into a bare concrete hallway. He unlocked a big wooden door. They all walked into a dusty room with things like tile and wood lying on the floor.

"We buy it without anything in it and then have to do everything to make it a home -- install a kitchen, a bathroom, windows, flooring, wall units for closets and storage." Lana said, "I made them tear out the walls between the bathing part of the bathroom and the toilet stall. The construction workers didn't understand why, but now I have a nice, big Western-style bathroom." It really wasn't interesting to look around the empty apartment, but Papa seemed to like looking at it, so Anastasia pretended to be interested.

Next they got back in the car and drove to the new *dacha* Lana and Sergei were working on in the country. Vegetable gardens grew around all the houses, some animals were penned in back yards, and people worked out in their yards. Anastasia looked around to see if there was anyone she recognized. She carefully walked around the new house and barn looking at everything. Then she saw her new Mama step in a patch of mud.

"Mama!" she shouted. "You have mud on your feet. They will spank you. You need to be more careful."

Her Mama didn't seem to understand her. She pointed to her shoes.

Mama very calmly wiped the mud on some grass and got most of it off but you could still tell she had stepped in the mud. Anastasia trembled to think how much trouble she would be in when they returned to the orphanage.

After they went to look at the new apartment and *dacha,* Mama and Papa took them back to the orphanage. They were just in time for dinner.

The next day and the one after that they played in the orphanage with their new parents, but the third day Sveta told them they would go with their new Mama and Papa to the park.

Anastasia didn't know what the park was, but Sveta sounded like it would be fun. It was always fun to play with her new parents. First they walked to a house near the orphanage. There Anastasia was allowed to pick some cherries and eat them. She shared them with Snijana. Their new Mama took her inside and dressed her in a very stiff, new, blue jumper with a white blouse. Then she gave her a hat. Anastasia loved the hat and the full skirt of the jumper. She twirled around and around. Next they put a little white dress on Snijana.

Anna went with them to the park. Lana told them to tell her if they needed anything. They walked across the street, between some houses, down another street and across an empty space. The walk was a little farther to the park than it had been from the orphanage to the house, and both Anastasia and Snijana were getting a little tired by the time they got there. But when they saw all the people, all the playthings, and all the trees and grass, they were excited. They couldn't decide what to play on first. Anastasia chose the merry-go-round. Their new Papa pushed them, but as soon as it started going fast, Snijana started crying. They had to stop the merry-go-round and take Snijana off. The new Mama took her to the swings and started pushing her. Snijana liked that so much Anastasia wanted to do it, too. She shouted at the new Papa to stop the merry-go-round, but he didn't seem to hear her. Finally Anna told him to stop it, and Anastasia jumped off and ran to the swings. Her new Papa pushed her and pushed her.

Finally her new Papa made her get off and pointed to his watch. Anna said it was time to go. They started walking back, but Anastasia needed to go to the bathroom. There was nowhere to go. Her new Mama took her to some weeds at the edge of the park, pulled down her pants and she went there. When they came back, Snijana said she needed to go, too. At first they did not hear her, but Anna told her new Mama and Papa that Snijana needed to go too. Mama took her to the weeds, but Snijana couldn't wait any longer. Just as Mama pulled down her pants she peed all over Mama's hands, her new dress and Mama's pants. Snijana cringed, waiting for Mama to yell at her and hit her, but she didn't. Mama frowned, took off Snijana's panties and wrung them out, then put them back on her, shook off her hands and walked back to the others. Anastasia giggled inside but didn't let it out in case she would be hit.

When they got back to the house, Mama washed her hands really well, took off Snijana's new clothes, and put the orphanage clothes back on her then changed her own clothes and washed her hands again. Anna's *Baba* (grandmother) washed Snijana's new clothes and hung them up to dry. Still nobody had been hit. The *Baba* put a pot in the yard, just around the corner from where the tables had been set up for dinner, and Snijana used it. She always had to pee a lot when she was nervous. Anastasia was glad she had a pot now.

Anastasia looked at the table. She didn't think she had ever seen so much food on one table before. She watched as Anna set the plates on the table and the *Tata* (grandfather) put chairs all around it. As Lana and the *Baba* put more food on the table, a car drove up. Sergei got out. He was a fun, laughing man, and Anastasia liked him almost as much as her Papa. Soon Papa lifted them into their chairs. Lana tied a big towel around Anastasia's neck, and her new Papa started filling her plate with food. Snijana was sitting next to her new Mama with a towel around her neck, and her Mama was filling that plate with food. They ate and ate and ate while the grownups talked.

After eating three plates of food Snijana got up and wandered around a little bit, then quietly went over to the corner of the porch and threw up. The new Mama and *Baba* Jumped up and ran to her .The new Mama picked her up and comforted her, *Baba* cleaned up the mess and they gave her some juice to drink. It was the most amazing thing Anastasia had ever seen. Snijana had gotten sick all over the floor, and they were cuddling and fussing over her. Anastasia couldn't recall anyone ever being cuddled and fussed over for being sick all over the floor. Snijana settled back into her Mama's arms and sat quietly for a long time.

After they finished eating, Sergei turned on the radio, and Anastasia danced with him. Then Snijana got up and started dancing. Anna danced with her and everyone laughed. After a while Snijana got tired and sat down. Her new Mama went into the house and got a stuffed bear that she gave to her. Snijana clutched it tightly while she sat on her new Mama's lap. Anastasia stopped dancing and tried to take the bear, but Snijana held it tightly. Then her new Papa gave Anastasia a huge, white stuffed dog. She played with it until they said it was time to go back to the orphanage. Papa carried Snijana, who was almost asleep, and Anastasia walked beside him wearing her new clothes and clutching her new, white dog. This was one of the best days of her life.

When they got back to the orphanage, they took off the new clothes and the nurses took them away, but the big white dog was put up on a shelf where nobody could touch it. It would stay where Anastasia could look at it and remember her new Papa every night.

Only a couple of days after they had gone to the park, Lana came back and explained that their Mama and Papa had to go back home to get everything ready for them to go there. Snijana was angry.

"They had said they would take us out of this place, but then they disappeared." she told Anastasia. "I don't like people come and make me feel good then go away. They are not really our Mama and Papa, no matter what anyone says. They said they would take us to a nice house like Lana's, but they didn't."

"They gave us nice toys and clothes," said Anastasia.

"But Sveta took them away when we got back to the orphanage," said Snijana. "It is no use wanting things, because you never get them anyway."

Chapter 11

When the foundations are being destroyed, what can the righteous do?
Psalm 11:3

Saturday found us back on the road to Kiev with Yaroslav, Anya and Julia, Rich and Betsy.

We slept that night in the sparsely furnished dormitory rooms at Yaroslav's university. We hesitated to use the bathrooms because they were so grimy and cockroach infested. The door to the room Betsy and I shared in the girl's dormitory did not lock, and this concerned us because of the high crime rate in Kiev. I slept very little that night.

The men's dormitory was even worse. It was beyond filthy. Trash overflowed everywhere and discarded pieces of furniture littered the rooms and hallways. Cockroaches swarmed through the rooms and halls in addition to the bathrooms. Whenever possible, University students lived at home or with relatives or friends when they went to school in Kiev. We could understand why.

On Sunday we went to the Pyrohiva Village, where dwellings and structures from several different villages had been combined to form a living museum demonstrating the traditions of different regions in Ukraine. The buildings interested Robert, especially the churches, which were built in different styles. Religion has always been stronger in Ukraine than in Russia and was not eradicated to the extent it was in Russia during Soviet times. One of the churches was preparing to hold services while we were there, but we had to leave before they started. Anya and Julia were most interested in the costumed Cossacks who were riding around, but to Anya and Julia's disappointment, we missed their trick riding demonstration.

Monday morning Anya and Julia acted as guides for Rich and Betsy while Yaroslav took us to the Ministry of Education, the ministry responsible for adoptions. The security guard stopped us at the door. Yaroslav explained what we wanted, and we all showed our identification. He sent us to an office on the third floor. In that office we asked for the person in charge of adoptions. They said she was out and asked several questions. The people who were there said it was useless to try to adopt the girls at the present time. They showed the usual disdain for anyone from outside Kiev and told us to come back later if we wanted to talk with the Director. Yaroslav told them we would be back.

The Director would not be back for several hours so we sat at a little café and talked about the economic and political situation in Ukraine. Yaroslav said things would be fine for people his age, but he was worried about people of his parents' generation who were having a hard time adjusting to the realities of the new situation. Yaroslav said we were in the most historic part of Kiev and suggested we look around. Only two blocks away he took us to the Golden Gate, the original gate to the walled city, built in 1017 by Yaroslav the Great, the founder of the first Kievian principality.

"Are you related?" we asked Yaroslav.

"I'm named after him but not a descendant," he told us laughing.

We walked down a hill to St. Andrews Cathedral, one of the most famous churches in the city, although it was closed for repairs. On the way back we stopped at St. Cyril's, one of the most beautiful in Kiev, built in 1146.

"This is the family burial site for Princess Olha's family. This is the tomb of Prince Svyatoslav Vsevolodovych, one of the people in the ancient Slavic literary masterpiece, *The Sayings of Prince Ihor*," Yaroslav told us.

Although we were not familiar with Slavic literature, thus unimpressed by seeing Prince Svyatoslav Vsevolodovych's tomb, we were impressed by the age of the church and the frescoes inside. The interior of the church is decorated with the original frescoes from the 12th century.

We rejoined Rich, Betsy, and the girls for lunch. Anya and Julia begged to ride the funicular, or cable railway, that connects the upper and lower city. Yaroslav used it regularly for transportation to school from his aunt's house and didn't find it very exciting, but the girls prevailed. On the short, steep ride we saw beautiful views of the river and city.

Late in the afternoon we returned to the Ministry of Education. It was almost closing time, and we had to leave Ukraine in the morning. Yaroslav boldly walked into the building without showing our identification. The guards rushed after us, but Yaroslav told them we had an appointment. We walked right into the director's office. She pointedly ignored us for some time. Yaroslav started talking to her as soon as she finished what she was working on. She accused him of being paid to help us and trying to get rich by charging Americans outrageous fees for helping them take poor Ukrainian children. She could understand some English, although she pretended she couldn't. At one point she asked about something I had said to Yaroslav that he did not translate.

I interrupted Yaroslav, saying, "We only want to help these children. We already love them after only just meeting them. We know they were meant to be our children, and we will love them like they are our biological children.

"It will help the people of Ukraine, too," I continued. "If these children

85

stay in the orphanage, they will grow up dependant on the system in Ukraine, and Ukrainians will have to pay higher taxes to support them. Then when they are sixteen they will be put out on the streets with a limited education and no chance of being productive citizens. If we adopt them, we can provide them with a good home and a good education, and they will have a chance to be productive, independent adults.

"It is distressing to me that Yaroslav is getting insulted for trying to help us with these two little girls, when he is doing all of this out of the goodness of his heart and has not even asked for anything." I concluded my speech.

I said all this to Yaroslav, but the Director understood most of it. She repeated that there was nothing to be done now because the procedures were not in place. We should wait until the procedures were in place. A bill for international adoption was before Parliament now, and she expected it to pass. We should come back when everything was arranged. We left, defeated, and boarded the plane dejectedly the next morning after another sleepless night in the University dormitory.

The trip back to the United States was a sad and frustrating one for us, even though we had a very nice canal boat tour and dinner with German friends of Rich and Betsy's in Amsterdam.

We stayed in touch with Lana, Anya, and Yaroslav on a regular basis for the rest of 1996. The laws about foreign adoption did pass in Parliament late that year. The first foreign adoption in Ukraine took place in October 1996. The parents were Canadians of Ukrainian descent. The new law had a requirement that children be on a waiting list for one year before they could be adopted. We suggested that Yaroslav's father contact the local representative and try to get an amendment added to the bill so that children who were already waiting would not have to wait another year before for adoption. Anya had taken a government class in the United States, so we asked her to explain to him how an amendment could work. They didn't have any luck getting an amendment passed.

That winter Lana suggested that she and Sergei adopt the girls then somehow give them to us, but we didn't have any idea how that could be worked out. American adoption lawyers told us that would be even more difficult than adopting them ourselves.

Even though the new adoption law had been passed, there were still no standard procedures in place six months later. Gradually our hope of getting the girls faded away. Lana wasn't sure what was happening concerning adoptions in Ukraine. I checked the State Department faxes on adoptions in Ukraine. The information was not encouraging. As time went by, I no longer wanted to talk about it. I still longed to hold Anastasia and Snijana, but I could not express it anymore because it hurt too much. Soon, I knew Luba would not be able to keep them in the orphanage. Anastasia would be five in April and would have to move on to the orphanage for older children. The orphanage for older kids was not a model orphanage, nor was it a warm, loving place like the orphanage for little children.

My mother, who had retired in Albuquerque two years before, wondered why I wanted to adopt children so badly. She had grown up as the middle child of nine, and my widowed grandmother was constantly taking in other children, sometimes for pay and sometimes just because they needed loving attention. When my mom married just after World War II, she would have liked a career in journalism or accounting, but at the time it was expected that women would give up their jobs to the men who had just come back from the war and create the baby boom. She did her share, adding three of us to that generation by 1954, and she was an excellent mother. Yet, to her, children represented hard work and sacrifice.

My mother couldn't imagine why, after what amounted to three rewarding and interesting careers in my early adulthood, I could truly want to dedicate myself to raising children. I knew it would be hard work and that at forty-five I didn't have the stamina and energy new mothers in their twenties do, but I had decided that was what I wanted to do with my life. When I explained my decision to my mother, she accepted it, as she had accepted my determination to travel around the world when I was twenty, and stopped making discouraging remarks. She did say, however, that they would be my children and my responsibility and I should not expect her to help raise them or to babysit whenever we needed someone to take care of them.

Chapter 12

Be strong and courageous. Do not be afraid or terrified because of them, for the Lord your God goes with you; he will never leave you or forsake you.
Deuteronomy 31:6

In the orphanage Anastasia looked at the white puppy high on the shelf in the sleeping room and cried herself to sleep, wondering why her Papa did not come and get her. She kept telling Pavlik that her Papa was coming and maybe he would take Pavlik, too, but she was beginning to think that it would never happen. But he had promised her. He had to come back.

When the older kids left after the summer program, Snijana moved into the same room as Anastasia. Now they could be together every day.

One day Anastasia found a really interesting looking bottle in the bathroom. She liked to collect interesting things, so she slipped it into her pocket. The substitute caregiver saw her and told her to put it back.

"It is okay. It is empty," she told the caregiver with her sweetest smile. "They let us have them when they are empty."

She slipped into the sleeping room and hid the bottle in her pillowcase. Later that week, when the regular caretakers were changing her sheets, they found the bottle.

"Anastasia, come here now!" called Sveta from the sleeping room.

She knew she had been caught. Sveta scolded her, spanked her, and made her sit in the corner. As she sat, she fumed at Sveta and told herself, "My Papa will come back and show them. They can't get away with this. He will come back and teach them a thing or two."

In September Pavlik stopped sleeping in the bed next to Anastasia. She missed their late night, whispered conversations, but Pavlik was too old for that orphanage now. One day, after music, Luba came and took Pavlik to her office. When he came back, he had exciting news for Anastasia.

"I don't have to go to the other orphanage. I will be going to live with Luba. I will go home with her at night and come back here to be with you during the day."

"But that is not fair," whined Anastasia. "I was going to ask this Mama who came to see me if she would take you, too. Why can't I go sleep at Luba's house, too."

"You are younger than I am," explained Pavlik. "I am too old to stay in this orphanage, but Luba doesn't want to send me to the next one."

"Why not?" asked Anastasia.

"Because I am different from other boys. Have you noticed when we go to the bathroom that I am different? I don't have that little hangy thing the other boys have. I have to go to the bathroom like a girl. That is why my Mama didn't want me and sent me to the orphanage."

Anastasia had noticed, but she had not thought about it before.

"Why does that mean you can't go to the other orphanage?" she asked.

"Luba thinks the other boys might tease me and be mean to me. I think having that little hangy thing is important as you get older."

Anastasia pouted in their corner.

"I will still be able to come and play with you during the day," Pavlik promised. "Every day I will come when Luba comes to work, and we can play together. Maybe when you are too old you can come to live with Luba, too. She really likes you."

But Anastasia still pouted.

At least he wasn't gone for good, like the people who were sent to the other orphanage. He came back with Luba every day and they could still play with each other. Because they had already been through all the lessons they taught in the four-year-old room, and because they were special friends, Anastasia and Pavlik got the run of the orphanage. As long as their care-givers knew where they were, they could go visit the kitchens, where they often begged snacks from members of the staff, and sometimes they could go outside and play on the broken down playground equipment while the others had lessons. They would run errands all over the orphanage and take messages to the maintenance man, who also sat at a table near the door and acted as a guard when he wasn't busy somewhere else, or to the nurses downstairs.

One day, after they had delivered a message to the nurse's office, Anastasia looked out the window. The apricot trees were full of fruit, there were flowers blooming in front of the orphanage, and she could hear birds sing-ing. "Let's go outside," she whispered to Pavlik.

"We didn't ask," said Pavlik. "We have to ask before we go outside."

"You get to go outside with Luba every evening," retorted Anastasia. "I never get to go out. I am going."

She marched out the front door of the orphanage with Pavlik behind her. They had barely made it out of the door, when the guard grabbed them and hauled them back inside.

"Where do you think you two are going?" he asked gruffly. He didn't like to have to get up from his desk because his *kist* hurt. Anastasia could tell he was angry. She just hung her head and looked sideways at him in a way she knew fooled most men. She might have gotten away with it, too, if Sveta hadn't come down the hall just then. When the guard had explained what they had been doing, Anastasia got another spanking, had to sit on her bed, and didn't get dinner. She looked at the dog on the shelf and begged her Papa to come back soon. Snijana came creeping into the sleeping room to try to comfort her, but Anastasia told her to go away. They did not allow her to leave the room for three weeks. Whenever she looked at the white, fluffy, dog she cried herself to sleep. It was as out of reach on that high shelf as her Papa was, wherever he went.

One day in midwinter Pavlik ran into the room. "There is a big truck outside. There are people from Canada with sweaters, toys and gifts. Come look."

Anastasia scampered to the window, where she could see the men unloading large boxes from the truck.

"Please, Sveta, can we see what they are doing?" Anastasia begged.

"Luba said I could go down. Please let Anastasia go with me," Pavlik begged.

Sveta said yes. Anastasia quickly bundled herself up, pulled on her boots, and they ran to the courtyard. Luba was talking with one of the men. Pavlik ran to her side, and Anastasia crept up beside the man. She slipped her hand into his and listened as he talked with Luba. When they went inside, she continued to hold his hand. They toured the orphanage, ending at Anastasia's room, which was next to Luba's office. Sveta insisted that Anastasia stay there but Anastasia begged her to let her go to the cloakroom to say goodby. Sveta relented. As he left, the man pulled a little silver ring from his pocket.

"This is for you," he said, handing Anastasia the ring. She held it tightly in her hand and, as soon as she could, placed it secretly under her pillow for safekeeping.

That afternoon, they presented a program for the visitors from Canada. Snijana loved programs. They dressed up in costumes from the storage room, and she got to stand in front of everyone and recite the nursery rhymes she had worked so hard to memorize. She and Yuri were the stars of the program, Yuri because he was good at memorizing the rhymes and Snijana because she glowed with a special joy when she was in front of a group. They had a great time, and after the program one of the women held Snijana on her lap. Snijana snuggled in and could have stayed there all day. She thought about how comfortable it had been to sit on her Mama's lap when they came for a visit, and once more she resolved that she would not trust these people who had made her believe that everything would be all right, then disappeared. Mama and Papa had been gone for months and months now. Lana came back often and talked about them, but Snijana didn't think she would ever see them again. She decided she should just forget about them.

Chapter 13

Be pleased, O God, to deliver me, O Lord, make haste to help me.
Psalm 70:1

By January 1997 we decided to go back to the New Mexico Department of Children Youth and Families. After a change of administration the department was being pressured to get at least some of the children in foster care into adoptive homes. We had first contacted them in 1989 and completed their program for prospective adoptive parents the winter of 1989-90. While large number of children were removed from their homes and placed in foster care, almost none were made available for adoption in the early 90's. When they were, we were often screened out as potential parents because we were not Hispanic or Native American. The social workers promised us that this time the policy of the department was strongly in favor of adoption and they could have children for us in just a few months.

We had been foster parents long enough to know that we could expect some psychological damage in any children we got. Because the policy of the department had been to make every effort to reunite families for several years, those who were finally released for adoption had been through several traumatic experiences. After children are abused, removed, placed in foster care or group homes, reunited, abused and removed so many times, at the very least they don't trust adults. This was one policy we had a great deal of trouble with as foster parents. Only the most resilient kids could survive. At least we knew the code words social workers use to describe the different behaviors children exhibit, and we knew what to ask for. We wanted children who could not be taken away from us, so we proceeded with the Children,

94

Youth and Families paperwork. In the meantime we continued as emergency foster parents, taking children who had been abandoned or abused, often in the middle of the night, and often dealing with ill or badly injured children.

CYFD approved all our paperwork in March. In April, the chairperson of a church building committee with whom Robert worked as architect gave him a magazine on international adoption. She had adopted two children from Russia and had followed our adoption attempts with interest. In that magazine three agencies advertised that they could help people adopt children from Ukraine. This gave me new hope. I called one of the agencies at random, called the International Children's Alliance or ICA. They told me that many people had tried to adopt children from Ukraine and that it would be very difficult to locate the girls we wanted to adopt. They could not guarantee they could help, but they had a form they would fax me. If I would fill out the form and send half the application fee, they would see what they could do. The form asked for the names of the children, name and location of the orphanage, and any other information we had, along with a description of our efforts so far. I had to send a fax to Lana to get some of that information.

While we were waiting for Lana's response, our CYFD social worker implied that we were very close to getting children through them. Should we pursue the Ukrainian adoption, with all the expense and uncertainty or just take the American kids, who needed us too. I knew Anastasia and Snijana were the girls I had seen in my dreams for so long. It was like living two lives, one in which we filled out paperwork for the adoption through CYFD and the other tenaciously certain that our kids were in Ukraine.

Robert wrestled with what direction we should go. One night we stayed awake talking for several hours.

"Do you really think things have changed?" I asked.

"I know that the new director of the Human Services Department, Heather Wilson is really trying to change things," he said.

"Yes, but how much can she change the entrenched bureaucracy? And can she do it in time for us?"

We ended by praying that God would give us some direction. The next morning we woke to a report on the clock radio that said, "Despite written statements that say there are no age restrictions on adoptions, it is very difficult for a couple more than forty years of age to adopt a child in the United States."

Robert had just turned fifty and I was forty-five. That decided it for him.

Lana's letter with the information we needed arrived about two weeks after my fax. I filled out the form, wrote a check, and sent it all off. I mailed it on a Friday. The following Tuesday there was a message waiting when I got to our office to call International Children's Alliance as soon as possible. I dialed the number, and when I gave my name, the person on the other end said to hold on. Two women got on the line. One introduced herself as Sue Orbin, the person who handles Eastern European adoptions. The other was Deborah McFaddin, the executive director of ICA.

"We received your form," Sue said, "and we know that adoptions are made in heaven, not on earth."

"This is a very interesting situation," said Deborah. "Not only were we able to find your girls, we have their pictures on our table and were about to match them up with a family. We have made call after call to this family but have not gotten a response. As soon as we saw your information we knew why. We have to match these girls up with you."

"There is one thing that bothers us though," added Sue. "There are three girls, not two. Did you know about the third?"

I was trembling at this point and could barely talk.

"They did mention a sister," I said. "Is she younger or older?"

"Younger," they said, which excited me. "Would you be willing to take all three?"

I was thoroughly convinced that these were our girls, and there was no question that we should take the third one. The chance of our girls' pictures and our form coming together in the same place at the same time in an agency in Washington, D.C., was astronomical. I had chosen the agency completely at random. The ICA representative in Kiev had never worked with this orphanage before but felt that these girls were highly adoptable and so had sent their pictures to Washington. And everything happened at the same time.

"Of course," I said. I didn't even think about consulting Robert; I knew he would agree, too.

Because the girls were cheerful, intelligent, beautiful and healthy, Sue and Deborah urged us to complete the paperwork quickly so we could adopt them before anyone else did. And because last year's paperwork would soon expire, we had to do everything over.

I had to attend a meeting of a non-profit board I was on that evening. I arrived still trembling. Robert was out of town, so I couldn't tell him about the call. Our friend Steve Herrera was at the same meeting, and he became the first to know that they had found our girls and we were proceeding with the adoption.

ICA faxed me a checklist of the paperwork needed and all the forms. I contacted Rainbow House immediately for an update of our home study. Rosalind went right to work on it and had it completed in a week. We requested a rush on all the other paperwork we needed. There had to be three copies of everything. Certain papers had to be kept separate and be stamped with their own set of official seals. Other pieces could be stapled together, provided the same person had notarized them, and sealed all at the same time. I made folders for each category of document and labeled them in large letters to avoid wasting time. We took everything we could to Rosalind at Rainbow House to be notarized so we could bundle it and save money. At the end of a week we had everything except New Mexico State Police clearance and medical forms. I began visiting our doctor's office daily until the nurse had the medical forms ready. I called the State Police office in Santa Fe. The head of the office there said that because the clearance for CYFD had been done so recently they could have new forms filled out within half an hour.

So with all the other forms in hand, we went to Santa Fe. Our first stop was at the State Police office to pick up the clearance. We went through the security check at the door and into the office of the person I had talked to. He was not there. Everyone who was there said that it would take at least two weeks to get the clearance. We asked to see the man's boss, but they said she was in an important meeting. The person we wanted to see would be back at 3:00 p.m.. All we could do was wait. I started to get upset, and perhaps a little loud. Robert took me by the arm, told them we would be back at 3:00 p.m. and led me out.

We went to the Capitol building and delivered the rest of the papers to the Secretary of State's office, then went to lunch while they placed the official seal of the State of New Mexico on them, guaranteeing that they were true and authentic documents. We picked up the papers and went back to the State Police office. We were a little early so we sat in the car listening to the radio for several minutes. All of a sudden Robert said, "It's time to go."

We got out of the car and walked toward the building. When we got to the door, we met Robert's cousin Debbie coming out the door. She introduced us to the man with her, an Assistant Attorney General with the Federal Attorney General's office, finished saying good-by to him then she asked us why we were there. We explained our situation and asked if she knew the man we were talking about.

"I'm his boss," she said.

She had been in that position for only three weeks, and we had no idea that she worked in that department. She led us into the office, told them to prepare the clearances for us, then took us to her office to talk while they were working on it. When the paperwork was completed, she signed it, we took it back to the Secretary of State's office, and we had all the paperwork done in only ten days. We sent the bundle of paperwork to ICA, and they sent it back, saying it had appostiles and it needed seals. Although we didn't know the difference and it wouldn't make much difference to most people in the United States, it does make a difference to the officials in the Ukrainian Embassy and Office of Foreign Affairs. So we went back to Santa Fe and got the right seal on the papers and sent them off again. ICA got the official seal of the United States Department of State and the Ukrainian embassy. They sent the paperwork to Ukraine, to be translated by an official translator and delivered to the Center for International Adoptions.

We hoped to leave for Ukraine almost immediately, but Sue from ICA called us shortly after the paperwork arrived in Ukraine and told us that the youngest Irina had not been put on the waiting list until October, so we had to wait until then to complete the adoption. They also told us not to have any contact with Lana because too many people working on the same adoption could really mess things up. We knew and trusted Lana while we didn't now anything about the people ICA might set us up with. We were a little offended, but we did not contact Lana. We had to wait!

Chapter 14

And the peace of God, which transcends all understanding, will guard your hearts and your minds in Christ Jesus. Philippians 4:7

In the bed next to Anastasia they put a little girl named Irina.

"This is your youngest sister," Sveta told her.

If this was her sister why had she never seen her before? She was only two years old and too little for the big kids' room. She wet the bed almost every night and couldn't feed herself without getting food all over her face. When the others took toys away from her, she didn't even fight back.

They made Anastasia take care of Irina. At mealtimes Anastasia would get her bib and tie it on for her and make sure she got her share of the food. Anastasia sat next to her and told her what she should do and what she should not do. At first Anastasia resented having to take care of Irina. She never spoke. Mostly she just watched what was going on. She didn't cry or yell or anything. She did pout though when things didn't go the way she wanted them to, so Anastasia knew she understood what was going on. There had been some kids in the orphanage who didn't even know what was going on. Irina wasn't one of those kids.

Irina gradually came to depend on Anastasia and adored her. Anastasia was proud that she could take care of the little sister she called Ira. Irina and Snijana looked alike, except that Snijana had blue eyes and Ira had unusual looking yellow eyes, so Ira must be her sister. Quiet, little Irina became Anastasia's special charge. At playtime, Anastasia made sure Irina had something to play with and that other kids didn't take it away from her. At night, Anastasia held her close until she went to sleep.

Irina could hold out longer than any of the other kids in the room. If she was full, she would hold food in her mouth for hours until she was hungry again. If Sveta wanted her to do something she didn't want to do, she would sit in her chair and refuse to do it, no matter what Sveta did to her. Anastasia was in awe of her ability to fake out the caregivers without saying a thing and without outwardly doing anything they could punish her for.

Shortly after Irina came, some of the kids who were Anastasia's age were taken to the other orphanage. In their place came a boy Snijana's age named Yuri and his two-year-old sister named Julia. They arrived late one afternoon, just at playtime. Right away Julia took a toy from Irina. Anastasia grabbed it away from her and returned it to Irina. Irina turned her back on Julia and kept playing with her toy. Julia tried to take it again, and Anastasia had to shove her away. Yuri came to his sister's aid, and Anastasia had to push him down to show him who was boss. As long as he knew, like everyone else already did, that she was boss of this room, everything would be fine. He didn't get the message very fast though. He got up and tried to take the toy from Ira. Anastasia pinched him hard on his arm. He grabbed his arm and backed away crying. She had established that she was in charge and would have no more trouble from him. Julia was a different story. She didn't give up so easily. Although she learned not to challenge Anastasia openly, she never really gave up.

Pavlik came to get Anastasia one afternoon, and they went outside to play. The leaves were falling and the day reminded her of that day Snijana had been attacked by the dog. She didn't think of Svetlana and Mikhail very often anymore, but this day reminded her of them.

"Please promise me you will never leave me," she begged Pavlik.

"You know I will be with you forever and ever," he said. "We will get married when we are grown up."

"I just don't want you to disappear like my big brother," she said. "You are the only big brother I have now, and I want to be with you always."

"I will be with you forever," he promised again.

He smiled at her, took her hand and they jumped into a pile of leaves the janitor had just raked up.

Chapter 15

I have set my rainbow in the clouds, and it will be a sign of the covenant between me and earth. Genesis 9:13

Waiting was hard. The adoption was never far from my mind, but our friends got tired of hearing about it, so I waited silently. In the summer as I reviewed our paperwork, I discovered that one of the questions had been answered incorrectly by my doctor. The question contained a double negative; she had apparently been confused by that and answered no when the answer should have been yes. She probably felt rushed since I had been pushing them to complete the forms. I called ICA, and an unfamiliar voice answered the phone. All the regular staff was out of the office at a convention of some sort, so I explained the situation. The person told me, "no one ever reads the paperwork that closely and they probably won't catch the error." She said she would mention it to Sue. I thanked her and promptly forgot about it in the rush of daily life.

Robert was working hard to keep his staff of five busy. They had several projects, and for once they were profitable projects. Our financial situation was finally in order, because we had been disciplined in both our spending and saving. The $50,000 in credit card debt we had the year before was com-pletely paid off.

Although ICA couldn't give us an exact cost for the adoptions, I calculated, from the information they had sent, that we would need about $28,000. We assumed we would be leaving around October 24, 1997, although October 4 was written on the picture they had faxed of Irina. We assumed that was the date it was sent to the Center for International

Adoptions and might be the date she was available. I calculated how we could get the money that I thought we needed by the end of October.

The Missions' Committee at church and some of our friends suggested they hold a fundraiser for us. We weren't sure it was suitable to accept money from other people to pay for our adoption, but one of the members of the Missions Committee, a former missionary herself, said that we would be giving others an opportunity to fulfill their Christian calling by contrib.-uting to the adoption fund. Like the fundraiser for the mission team two years before, it would be an ice cream social, silent auction and concert. Steve Herrera, whom we had asked to be Anastasia's godfather, would perform the concert. Steve is a composer of Christian music and does inspirational concerts for youth around the country. Many members of the congregation donated deserts for the ice cream social or sales items for the auction. We brought in some antique furniture we really didn't need. Artists with whom Robert had worked over the years donated several beautiful pieces. I wanted to bid on some of the art pieces but had to restrain myself. The concert was great, with a combination of funny, moving, and inspirational songs. We taped it so the girls could one day know how much the wonderful people at the church had done for them. In all, we raised more than $6000 that night.

Sue asked us to decide what we would name the girls. We decided to hyphenate our last names with Robert's name first, even though in the traditional Hispanic culture of New Mexico, having the father's last name first means that the parents are not married. Anastasia would remain Anastasia. Her middle name would be Marie, after my grandmother.

Snijana is the name of a heroine in a Ukrainian folk tale that is essentially the same as our story of Snow White, but Snow White wouldn't work very well in the United States. It is a tradition in my family to name the oldest girl after her father, and I have a cousin named Jana, the Polish form of John. We decided to take the Sni off the beginning of her name and add mine to the end, so her name became Janalyn. We played with quite a few middle names but decided Suzanne would be a good choice. She would have three Aunt Sues, so it would satisfy every branch of the family.

Until the last minute, we were going to leave Irina's name Irina, but in the end we chose to name her after my mother Lydia. Her name became Lydia Irene.

In August we went on a short vacation, and all I could think of was what might go wrong before we could get to Ukraine and get our girls. When we returned, I called Sue.

"Is everything all right with our adoption?" I asked.

"Everything is still on track," Sue replied

"What will happen if someone else tries to get the girls? Are they healthy? Is everything okay at the orphanage? I want to talk with Lana so she can see if everything is going well."

"Our representative in Ukraine is on top of things. No one can get the girls until October. The director has made it clear that all three girls need to be adopted together. There are still no guarantees. Things do go wrong in international adoptions, but we are doing everything we can to assure that you get your girls. Don't call Lana, because if she gets involved the Center for International Adoptions might think there is someone else trying to adopt the girls. They might think someone is trying to make money by getting you the girls, or any number of other things. What is going on there?"

I explained that we had been on vacation for a few days and that I just kept thinking of everything that could go wrong.

"Promise me you will not go on any more vacations until after you have the girls," Sue said.

I promised. I would work hard and not allow myself any spare thinking time.

That summer we remodeled our office building. Our secretary resigned in the middle of the remodeling process, and we hired a new one in September, just before moving back into the office. Within hours after we hired her, I got a call from her fiancé. He had planned a surprise trip to New York City for her as a birthday present and by taking this job she had ruined his plans. I told him to go ahead and let her start work, then take her to New York. Maria's first week on the job she helped move the furniture back into the office and rearranged all the files. Then she went to New York. The next Monday, October 6, I went into the office prepared to begin her orientation. I sat at my desk to go through a few papers first, when the phone rang. Maria paged me. It was Sue at ICA.

She said, "You have to be in Ukraine as soon as possible. There is a German couple who want to adopt your girls. You need to get there before they do."

"Germany is a lot closer to Ukraine than New Mexico is," I said, "But okay, we will try to get there before they do."

"Our travel agency will fax you your itinerary. Tom, here in our office, will fax you information on how much cash you need to take with you and the amount of our fees. You will need to take brand-new $100 bills. Overnight us your passports and an extra passport photo and we will walk your visas through and overnight them back to you so you will have them before you leave on Wednesday."

My mind was racing. "We leave on Wednesday. Today is Monday. Robert doesn't have an extra passport picture. The money I was expecting to use won't be available until the end of October. We don't even have money belts to carry all this cash." After months of waiting everything was going too fast.

"You will need gifts for all the people who help you. Get nice gifts for the Directors of the Orphanage and Center for Adoptions and the Judge. You will need several other gifts, too."

My head was spinning now. I told Maria she was on her own while I went shopping. Robert immediately began arranging things with his clients and employees so he could be gone for three weeks, then went to get another passport picture taken. The faxes arrived and we needed $8000 more than my calculations had shown. Some of it would be sent to ICA in Washington, but a large part of it had to be cash we would carry with us to Ukraine. We arranged for cash advances on our credit cards, borrowed some money from my mother, and Tom arranged for a scholarship from ICA. I called our bank to arrange to get $18,000 in new $100 bills. They didn't have it on hand but said they could get it for us the next day when we explained the situation. We had a good relationship with the bank vice president and had told him about the adoption earlier. I called Wally Barnes, a friend from church, and asked if he could take us to the airport. Somehow it was all coming together despite the mad scramble and the lack of the schedule, goals, and organizational plan we usually make before any major undertaking.

Sue called again on Monday and gave me some more instructions about how to behave when we got to Ukraine. "Our people there will take care of everything. Things are sometimes done differently in Ukraine than they are here. You can trust them to do what is best and to work everything out. Just go along with them and do what they say, and everything will be fine."

In between buying gifts, packing, and getting the money together we called friends. Jaynie Hakeem, a very close friend who would be Irina's godmother, and Ken, one of our employees, organized a prayer force that extended across the nation. Fourteen churches and hundreds of individuals prayed for us. And we were praying as well.

Robert worked all night Tuesday, writing out instructions, finishing reports, and composing letters to clients while I packed; somehow by Wednesday morning we were ready to leave -- except that our passports and visas had not been delivered. We called ICA and they called UPS. UPS said they were in Albuquerque. We called the Albuquerque office and they said the delivery person had them in his truck. They couldn't reach the delivery person until he got back to the center, sometime around 10:00 a.m. Our plane left at 10:00 a.m. Wally arrived to take us to the airport, but we couldn't leave without our passports. Anxious to have the passports, Robert went back to the office in case they had tried to deliver them there. He found a delivery slip on the front door, placed there fifteen minutes after he had left, around 6:00 a.m. ICA had put our home address on the package. They still had one copy of the label. Why had UPS decided to deliver it to the office?

At 9:00 a.m., as the delivery person was on his way back to the package center, he decided to make one more try to deliver the package to the office.

Robert was there. He called me immediately. I was on the other line with ICA. I told them we had the package and hung up. Wally and I jumped into his vehicle. We picked Robert up in the parking lot outside the office and made it to the airport with forty-five minutes to spare. We never did find out how the label on the UPS package got changed to our office address. All we could think of was that the other address was not readable and since we do have an account with UPS they found that address and delivered the package there.

We flew from Albuquerque to Dallas, and from Dallas to Frankfurt, Germany. In Frankfurt we changed clothes, because we knew we would be going straight from the airport to the Center for International Adoptions.

As we landed in Ukraine, I looked out the window and saw the shadow of the airplane on the clouds. Three bright, full circle, concentric rainbows encircled the shadow. I pulled Robert over to the window and showed him. I knew that was a sign from God that we would get our girls.

Little did we know the long and winding path we would have to take before that happened.

Chapter 16

I will not leave you as orphans. I will come to you. John 14:18

The airport was essentially unchanged from our visit a year and a half before: same water stained ceiling tiles, same broken floor tiles. If anything it was a little dirtier. The place felt familiar to us, giving us a sense of security. We dragged our suitcases out of the pile and got in line. We moved slowly up the line until there were only three people in front of us. Then a guard stopped the next person in our line and escorted several VIPs to the plywood customs booth. We had to wait patiently for them to be cleared before the line moved again.

As we dragged our suitcases out of the customs area, we saw a sign that said Habiger-Doxon. A good-looking young man who introduced himself as Yuri, our translator, held the sign. He introduced us to Svetlana, the ICA representative in Kiev. Yuri explained that he would be with us everywhere that we went in Kiev, and if we needed anything, all we had to do was ask. Svetlana had hired a car to take our luggage to the apartment where we would be staying while her husband Misha drove us to the Center for International Adoptions. This was a much better beginning than last year, and Svetlana seemed to have everything under control. Yuri was an excellent communicator, helping us feel connected even across the language barrier.

The Center for International Adoptions had moved to a different building. We drove into a little dirt motor court surrounded by three and four-story buildings. We entered the office building by a side door, and the guard there greeted Svetlana and nodded at us. The building reminded me of the old high school in which my father had taught in the 1950's. There were wooden school desks in various places in the hallways, where people would be expected to wait, wainscoting, and dusty green paint. We climbed the wide wooden steps to the third floor, where Svetlana found her contact and told her we were there.

Svetlana asked us to wait in the hallway while she went into the office. After several minutes Svetlana returned and ushered us into the office of the director. The director was a short, stocky woman with dyed red hair. There are two types of red dye common among Ukrainian women, orange-red and purple-red. She used the purple variety. We explained that we wanted to adopt these three girls. The director remembered seeing us the previous year and asked, "Have you been here before, trying to adopt children?"

If we told the truth she might reject us because we had not followed the rule and waited. If we didn't tell the truth, she might throw us out for lying.

Finally Robert said, "We were here a year and a half ago, trying to adopt the two older girls. We did not know about the youngest then."

I added, "The director of the orphanage did not mention Irina. She probably hoped that at least Anastasia and Snijana would get adopted, even if we couldn't adopt Irina."

We were very anxious about telling her this, but it turned out that we did the right thing.

A staff member tried to get us to look at pictures of other children in their book but we insisted we wanted these girls. After we said that, they went into an inner office and talked.

When she came out, the Director said, "We were not aware you were coming and have no knowledge of your qualifications for adoption. Come back tomorrow after we have had an opportunity to review the documents, and we will give you our decision."

We were very disappointed and angry that ICA had not done their job. We were worried that the Center for Adoptions would refuse to do anything and that all the effort and expense we had gone to would come to nothing. At the time we did not understand the Ukrainian way of doing business. Although the director said that they did not know we were coming and had to review the documents, the staff was probably discussing whether they would come out better by allowing the German couple or us to adopt the girls. The contacts made by the German couple and by Svetlana had probably been made through different members of the staff, and the director wanted to discuss the situation with all of her staff.

Svetlana took us to our "home" in Kiev, a four-room apartment in the same building where Svetlana lived. This was a luxury penthouse in Ukraine. A divorced woman, her two sons, and her father, who had come in from the country for a few days, occupied the apartment. It seems her former husband also lived there when he wasn't at his girlfriend's apartment because housing is expensive and hard to come by in Kiev. Since her father was there, we slept in the TV and sewing room. Our hostess was a remarkable cook, an accomplished seamstress, and a good carpenter. We were exhausted from the flight, disappointed and disoriented by the unexpected rejection at the Center for Adoptions, and very grouchy. We weren't very good guests for our host family. In fact, we barely responded to them. We ate the food they gave us, thanked them, and went to our room. They probably thought we were arrogant and pompous Americans rather than just being drained and supremely disappointed.

In the morning Svetlana and Yuri took us back to the Center for

International Adoptions. We couldn't meet with the Director right away, so we sat at the little wooden school desks in the hallway. It seemed like hours but was probably only about forty-five minutes. We finally went into the director's office. After about half an hour of discussion, most of which was not translated for us, the director agreed that we were qualified to adopt children and could visit the orphanage. Another hour passed while they prepared the paperwork. Then we had to take the papers to the lawyer's office. Yuri sat with us in the car while Svetlana ran in to get the letters she needed. We waited and waited and waited. After two hours Svetlana came back out with the letters and explained that the printer had been broken so the lawyer had been unable to print the letters we needed until a repairman came. With the letters in hand, we went to the notary, where we waited another hour in their waiting room to get everything notarized. Then we were ready to go to Kirovograd, except that it was Friday. We would be unable to do any business in Kirovograd over the weekend, so we decided to spend it in Kiev.

On Saturday afternoon, we walked with Yuri to a department store not far from Svetlana's apartment. The walk took us past shabby storage yards and a beautiful park. This contrast between drab, rundown business places and beautiful recreational spaces was one of the many contrasts we saw in Ukraine. The department store was a big concrete and tile building with three floors packed with things for sale. Each section was run as a different shop. There were at least ten different proprietors on each floor. We started just by looking around at the various things that were for sale. We paid careful attention to what Yuri was looking at because he was one of the people we would need to buy presents for. Then we decided to buy a couple of scarves.

We found a sales person and had Yuri talk with her about what we wanted. Prices were set, so there wasn't any bargaining, but it still took quite a bit of conversation to select the scarves. After the selection was made, the salesperson wrote out a slip of paper, and we were to take that and the scarves to the cashier. The cashier added up the price on her calculator and made change from her moneybox. We made several other purchases, includeing a gold watch for Yuri, although we did not tell him it was to be his. Each time we expected the salesperson to walk to the cash register and take our money, and Yuri had to remind us how it was done. We spent about three hundred dollars and still didn't get all the gifts we would need.

Knowing Robert designed churches, Yuri suggested a sightseeing tour of Ukrainian church architecture for Sunday. The first stop was St. Sophia, the best-known church in Kiev. It was originally built around 1017, although there had been many additions and restorations since then. In fact, we had been unable to see it the previous year because they were restoring it. We were able to see some of the original frescoes, which are still intact after more than one thousand years. At that time Robert bought slides of the church and frescoes from a sidewalk vendor for about ten dollars, so we knew what we would see inside.

Next we went to the ancient monastery of Lavre. We entered through a gate under an onion-domed cupola and walked along the cobbled streets. The monastery is still in use, so only specifically designated places are open to visitors. The church and several other buildings also have gold leaf-covered onion domes, while all the other stucco buildings have green metal roofs. It was quite beautiful. We climbed to the top of the bell tower, which has 240 steps and is the tallest structure in Kiev. From there we had a magnificent view of the city and the Dnieper River.

On the same river bluff, the Soviets had built a statue to friendship between Ukraine and Russia. It is a giant woman holding up a sword, looking toward Moscow. I think it is supposed to be Mother Russia, and I am sure the implications of what would happen if the Ukrainians did not accept this "friendship" were not lost on anybody. The monument is made entirely of titanium so it shines very brightly on the hillside. There have been suggestions that Ukraine could be very wealthy if they would just dismantle the titanium lady and make golf clubs out of her. When they were building the statue, the sword extended higher than the monastery bell tower but the Ukrainian people insisted that nothing could be taller than the bell tower or it would have disastrous consequences for Ukraine, so the builders shortened the sword. It is now just slightly shorter than the top of the bell tower.

We also visited the catacombs under the monastery. Before we went, Yuri asked me, "Do you know what is down there?"

"It is catacombs with people buried in them, isn't it?" I asked.

"Yes," he replied. "But I took one family down there and the woman did not know there would be bodies there. She ran out screaming. I just wanted to make sure you wanted to go."

"I want to go," I said.

I was actually disappointed that we could not go very deep into the catacombs because a religious service was taking place. At one time the catacombs went on for miles, but they are mostly filled in or blocked off now.

In 945 AD three Viking brothers and their sister sailed down the Dnieper River and founded the city of Kiev. A bronze ship with the three brothers standing in the center and the sister riding on the prow, her hair waving in the wind, now stands as a monument to the quartet. We visited that after leaving the monastery. It is traditional for wedding parties to visit the monument and for brides to leave their flowers there. Two wedding parties visited while we were there. It was a beautiful, clear autumn day. Walking through the clean, well-maintained park with Yuri and discussing his dreams for the future cheered us up immeasurably.

On Monday morning, with Svetlana's husband Misha as driver, we headed to Kirovograd in a heavy fog. As we drove, the fog turned to rain. At first Robert and I recognized landmarks along the way. Then we started seeing things we were sure we had never seen before.

"Are we going the right way?" I whispered to Robert.

"I don't think we went this way last year," he whispered back. "I don't think he has a map."

"Lana told us last year that you can't get a map to Kirovograd because the Soviets didn't want people to find it."

"We are definitely on the wrong road," Robert said quietly.

There was really nothing we could do about it, because we really didn't know the right roads to take and Yuri wasn't with us. Misha spoke a little English but not enough to discuss whether we were on the right road or not.

As we drove through one village a man at the side of the road waved his arm and Misha stopped. It was a policeman, and we had been caught in a speed trap. The policeman didn't have a car. He just stood at the side of the road flagging down cars.

"What would happen if we had not stopped?" I asked Misha.

"They shoot us," he said matter-of-factly.

After a six-hour trip, we finally arrived in Kirovograd. We had come in from a different direction than we had the year before, leading us to believe that perhaps we had taken a different, somewhat longer route.

Misha just happened to park in the driveway of the Malyuta family's apartment while Svetlana went to the hotel next door to get our interpreter. They wouldn't let us go up and say hello. By this time Anya was attending college in the United States and Yaroslav was teaching at the local teacher's college, but Julia might have been home.

The interpreter Svetlana hired had not spoken English in five years, and she had learned British English, so our accents confused her. We had to say everything at least twice, and when someone was trying to tell us something they would talk for a minute or two then she would tell us one sentence. We didn't understand everything she said either. This was such a big contrast to Yuri, and to the English-speaking people we knew in Kirovograd that we began to get angry and confused again. We were tired from the extended road trip and upset at the constant delays.

When we were ready to go, the car wouldn't start. Misha tried to fix the car while we sat trying to make conversation with the interpreter. She was one of the shyest people we had met in our entire stay in Ukraine. She didn't even seem to like talking with Ukrainians. Finally the car started again, and we were on our way.

The interpreter directed us to the parking lot behind the courthouse, then led us all in a side door and down the stairs to the office of the Orphanage Inspector. The Inspector took our papers and granted approval for us to visit the orphanage. She told us that in order to adopt children, the Orphan's Council, which met on Tuesdays, must first approve the documents then the City Council, which met twice a month on Wednesday, had to approve them. The City Council would need the approval of the Orphan's Council at least a week before they met. That meant our papers would need to be approved the next day at the Orphan's Council meeting or our process would be delayed for three weeks. Svetlana had never worked in a city where the City Council had to approve adoptions.

Luba was not at the orphanage, and no one else could grant us permission to see the girls. We insisted on walking around the corner to Lana's parents' house, so she would at least know we were in town. Her father was delighted to see us. Our interpreter couldn't translate much of the excited conversation, but we did manage to communicate that we would be at the orphanage. We were determined that we had to have a different translator if we were going to get anything done. Since we couldn't proceed with anything until Luba was at the orphanage, we convinced Misha and Svetlana to take us back to the Malyuta family apartment, where we left a note saying we needed help finding a better interpreter. We couldn't explain this to Svetlana, because the only person who could interpret our need to her was the interpreter we wanted replaced. Because of our previous experience in Kirovograd, we felt we knew the situation better than Svetlana. While she seemed to think it would be difficult to get a highly proficient English interpreter in a small provincial city like Kirovograd, we knew better. In fact, the three best English interpreters we met in all of our stay in Ukraine were from Kirovograd.

The next stop was the apartment where we would stay. We drove to a part of town we had not seen before. The streets were in even worse repair here than they were in most of the city. There were huge potholes filled with water from the recent rain. The concrete buildings seemed a little more brown than the cool grey of the newer buildings. There was an unpleasant smell in the air, and we didn't see any parks or stands of trees like there were in many other parts of Kirovograd. We stayed only long enough to meet our hostess, a close friend of our interpreter, and drop off our luggage.

Svetlana called and determined that Luba had returned to the orphanage and would give us permission to see the girls. We returned to the orphanage and all went into the cloak room where we sat on little benches. Luba told the caregivers to bring the girls out. First Irina shuffled out of the day room, looking at her feet and starting to whimper softly. We had not seen her before, and she did not know what to expect. I picked her up and gave her a piece of candy. She snuggled into my lap, not looking at anything else. She refused to let Robert get anywhere near to her. Then Sveta led Snijana out. They had been somewhat reluctant to let us see the girls because Snijana had a temperature of 40° C or about 104° F. They had taken her out of bed and dressed her for the visit, but bright red spots glowed in the center of each cheek and her eyes were glazed. She recognized us and hugged us and sat on my lap next to Irina.

Finally Anastasia was ready. She walked out the door, took one look at Robert, yelled "Papa" and ran and jumped into his arms. "My papa came back for me. I knew he would. This is my Papa," she kept saying.

Through her tears Svetlana said, "I have never seen a parent meeting like this."

Everyone was crying.

Svetlana motioned for us to sit on the low bench, and she took our picture. We were just getting up when Lana ran in the door. She threw her arms around Robert and me. "You must come to dinner at my parents' house," she said.

"We would love to, but Svetlana is providing our transportation and has a place for us to stay," we responded.

Lana turned to Svetlana, speaking in rapid Ukrainian. Svetlana was reluctant at first, but Lana talked her into it.

"She will bring you. I told her Sergei will fix the car," Lana said and rushed back out as quickly as she had come to prepare the meal.

The papers that had been signed off so far, first in the Center for International Adoptions, then with the Orphanage Inspector, and finally by Luba, had been to approve us as prospective adoptive parents and to give us permission to visit the orphanage to select children to adopt. Now that we were approved and the children officially selected, we had to get permission to adopt these children. First Luba would have to approve, next the Orphanage Inspector, then the Orphan's Council and City Council, and finally the Center for International Adoptions. Luba began preparing her permission as soon as we left for Lana's.

At Lana's I helped serve the meal and in the process managed to ask Lana to explain our problems with the interpreter to Svetlana. Toward the end of the meal the telephone rang. It was Luba saying that the orphanage inspector had found a discrepancy in the papers. Svetlana immediately called the Inspector who asked if I had any health problems. We insisted I didn't but carefully examined our copy of the papers. We found the mistake on my medical form that I had forgotten all about. Svetlana said we would have to try to get the error in the papers corrected. I didn't know who to be mad at: myself, my doctor, ICA or the whole world. I think I settled on the whole world.

We went to the apartment where Svetlana had arranged for us to stay. She would stay at the hotel by the Malyuta's but, like most places in Ukraine, they had one price for Ukrainians and another for foreigners. The hotel would cost us several hundred dollars a night, even though it was not that nice a place. Generally, it worked out better for families who came to adopt to stay with a local family in their apartment. We paid thirty dollars a day for room and board, which was generous by their standards and quite reasonable by ours.

We found this apartment unsatisfactory even after our previous visit to Ukraine. While it may have been a little cleaner and better organized than the University dorm rooms, the bathroom smelled worse than the outdoor latrine at Lana's parent's house. The water was off most of the day, and the electricity went off for several hours each day. The whole house smelled of smoke and our hostess served us only sausage and butter sandwiches for dinner, although that wasn't too bad because we had eaten quite well at Lana's. Svetlana tried to call ICA in Washington, D.C. from their house, but it was Columbus Day and nobody was in the office.

Late that evening I called my doctor's office. "This is Lynn Doxon," I said. "I am calling from Ukraine. Is the doctor's nurse there?"

The receptionist said, "Could you call back later? She is eating her lunch."

"I am calling from Ukraine," I repeated. "Is there anyone there who could help me?"

The receptionist said, "Is that long distance?"

"Yes," I said, rolling my eyes. "It is very long distance. It is almost on the other side of the world. It is part of the former Soviet Union. Is there someone there who can help me with getting some paperwork corrected?"

"Just a minute," she said and put me on hold for about five minutes.

Finally my doctor's nurse came on the line and apologized for the delay. I explained what had happened and that we needed a new form, needed to get it properly notarized and sealed and delivered to Ukraine as soon as possible. She agreed to take care of it. I went to bed feeling quite good.

About midnight Sue called from ICA. They were in emergency mode in Washington, trying to get the paperwork corrected, legalized, and shipped to us as quickly as possible. I explained our problems with our interpreter and apartment to Sue. She promised to relay the message to Svetlana. After that, I didn't sleep until about 4:00 or 5:00 a.m., which wasn't going to make me look any healthier the next day.

The next morning we met with the Inspector. We tried to explain that the answer on the paper was a mistake, my doctor was already correcting it, and we would have the corrected papers soon. After a long discussion, she said that she would proceed with the papers the way they were. We went back to the apartment and ate some more sausage and butter sandwiches before returning to sit on benches in the hall outside the Inspector's office, waiting for the results of the Orphan's Council meeting. After about an hour, the inspector came out and said their lawyer had told her not to proceed, so the Council had not considered the case. We waited another hour for Svetlana to get another chance to talk with the inspector. Svetlana finally said she would leave our paperwork with the inspector. She asked us to use any influence we had with our friends to get the City Council to hear the case the day after the Orphan's Council approval. We talked with Lana and left a note at the Malyuta's apartment. Svetlana told us through the interpreter that we should go back to Kiev and try to get the paperwork taken care of there. We would have the corrected document faxed to Svetlana and try to get it legalized through the American consulate. If that did not work, we would have to wait for the FedEx delivery from the United States.

After naptime we were allowed a visit with the girls. Irina spent the entire time snuggled against my chest, except when we made her stand up to take her picture. Although Irina was nearly three years old, she still did not talk, was only thirty inches tall and weighed only twenty-three pounds. She trembled when we picked her up too quickly, didn't smile, didn't cry loudly, didn't run and was generally totally silent. She loved to be cuddled and observed everything very closely with those intense, amber eyes, so we didn't feel she would have any attachment or intellectual problems. We were confident that the speech would come after she had enough attention.

Anastasia would have nothing to do with me and only played with Robert. She liked to play horsie with him or put on his hat and coat and pretend to be him. Papa belonged to her and she was jealous when he paid attention to the other girls. Snijana was feeling a little better and wanted to play. We handed out the dolls and stuffed animals we had brought with us. Snijana immediately traded the white teddy bear we had given Irina for her brown bear. Irina didn't seem to mind. She would take whatever she got to play with. Snijana tried the same thing with Anastasia, but it didn't work. Anastasia shoved her away and scolded her in rapid Ukrainian. Irina cried when it was time for us to leave. I had held her for almost an hour since she had craved physical contact and attention. We did not tell the girls we were leaving Kirovograd again. We just told them that we would not be able to visit them for a couple of days.

Chapter 17

Lord, let your mercy be upon us, as we place our trust in you. Psalm 33:22

Although we were deeply disappointed and angered by the delay, Svetlana assured us that we were lucky to have caught the mistake early because it could easily be corrected at this point. If the judge had found it in the last step of the adoption, it might have meant that we could not adopt the girls at all.

We returned to Kiev on Wednesday. We rushed straight to Svetlana's apartment and picked up the faxed medical form, then drove to the foreign sector of Kiev and waited at a little picnic table, where Yuri met us. After speaking with Svetlana for a little while he told us, "When we get the paperwork taken care of and you return to Kirovograd, you will live with Lana and Lana will be your interpreter."

We were relieved. The woman who was our hostess probably needed the money so badly that she had used it for her family and fed us only sausage. I was a little sorry that she would not have this much-needed source of income but not sorry enough to subject myself to those conditions again.

"No one could explain this to you in Kirovograd, because the only interpreter was the one being dismissed, and she was a friend of your hostess." Yuri explained. "Svetlana arranged this over the telephone with Lana." Our confidence in ICA was restored at this point. They hadn't missed the fact that the interpreter and the apartment were substandard.

When the Consulate opened, I was concerned about the long line of people waiting to get in, but Yuri assured us that we would have no trouble because we were Americans. We were immediately admitted to the anteroom where the guards do security searches. They let Svetlana come in with us because she was helping us, but we would have to do the talking this time. After my purse and Robert's backpack had been searched and Svetlana had turned in her bag and coat, we entered the waiting room of the consulate. We stood in a short line in front of the bulletproof windows until it was our turn. I explained what we needed to the Ukrainian clerk. She immediately got a very pleasant American man who explained that he could notarize my signature. He was clear that he could not guarantee that it was a true document; he was just notarizing my signature. I wrote across the top of the paper that this was a true and accurate statement and signed it. He notarized the signature. My doctor's signature on the correction was also notarized.

We took the paper to the Ministry of Foreign Affairs where they said they could not legalize the document because the American Consulate did not guarantee it. The American Consulate could not guarantee it because it did not have the seal of the State of New Mexico, which basically only says that the notary who notarized the doctor's signature is a legal notary in New Mexico. We now had to wait for the original papers to be shipped to us. ICA had already gotten all the seals and guarantees in the United States and shipped it by Fed Ex overnight, but that did not mean we would get it the next day. They couldn't guarantee how soon it would arrive.

We went back to the apartment in Svetlana's building. Our hostess's father had left by this time, so we slept in the older son's room and they were able to use the sewing and TV room. The apartment was on the east side of the Dnieper River and had a panoramic view of the city, including the Lavre monastery, titanium lady, and sports stadium. It was a great location and among our best accommodations in Ukraine, although we were in no mood to appreciate that fact.

Robert was very angry with me for not having corrected the problem during the summer so we wouldn't have to go through this. I was upset with myself for having forgotten about it and upset with Robert for being so angry with me. We were depressed by the delay and the dreary weather. We had not seen the sun since leaving New Mexico, and I tend to get depressed if the weather is cloudy for more than a couple of days at a time. This is one of the reasons I like living in New Mexico. A Ukrainian autumn was almost more than I could take. The brightest spot was the excellent cooking of our Ukrainian hostess.

On top of everything else, it was cold. In Soviet countries they take centralization very seriously. When they say they have central heating, they mean central heating for the entire city. There are huge boiler plants that provide all the hot water for all the heat in the city. They fire them up in late October and turn them off in April, no matter what the weather. The temperature of any apartment depends on the distance from the heating plant, the floor the apartment is on, and the direction the apartment faces. Now we understood Lana's pleasure at having an apartment that faced northwest and was on the fourth floor. It was able to pick up a little, but not too much, heat from the late afternoon sun and stay reasonably warm through the night. It also had several apartments above it to help hold in the heat and several below to help provide heat. In contrast the apartment we stayed in was on the next to highest floor, and although it faced west, it was always damp and cold. We had never been so cold as we were in those huge, concrete apartment towers.

Robert and I had lost sight of the vision of taking the girls home. We had expected it to be a simple matter of completing all the formalities because the laws were in place and we had ICA to help us. After a full week in Ukraine we had gotten nothing done. We were quite aggravated and irritable. Robert and I spent most of Thursday wrapped in blankets reading or playing solitaire and brooding on the difficulty and discomfort.

When Yuri came over on Friday to tell us the FedEx plane had not landed due to bad weather, we spent the whole evening complaining to him. We whined about the poor translator and accommodations in Kirovograd. We griped that they hadn't let us contact our friends sooner; then they completely changed their attitudes after they met Lana and asked us to have Lana use her influence to help us. We told him that the problems should have been taken care of sooner, and that we didn't believe that the papers could actually be on their way by Wednesday. We needed a release and completely unburdened ourselves to Yuri. That was a mistake!

Sue called on Saturday and said everyone inboth Washington, D.C. and Ukraine was getting upset and thinking we hated ICA. Apparently Yuri had talked with Svetlana, Svetlana had talked with Irina, the ICA interpreter in Washington, and Irina had talked with Sue. Each time the problem had gotten a little bigger. We were more upset with each other and the circumstances we were in than anything else but Svetlana was taking it personally. We would have preferred to stay in Kirovograd with Lana while Svetlana came back and took care of the papers. Sue talked with us for some time and helped us put things back in perspective. She explained that Svetlana really didn't need us to be there but she really did need to save face with the people she had hired as hostess and interpreter by taking us back to Kiev. She assured us that the papers had been properly legalized and put on the FedEx plane on Tuesday evening and should have arrived on Friday. We apologized to Sue and Svetlana and vowed to be more careful what we said. I had forgotten that this process was all in God's hands and that it would turn out right in the end. Robert and I both have a tendency to see what needs to be done and do it. Just sitting and waiting for other people to work things out was very difficult. We found it interesting that we could be so bored and so nervous at the same time.

On Saturday it was cold and rainy. We spent the morning in the apartment, but Yuri convinced us to go out shopping in the afternoon, rather than sit around brooding. Misha dropped us off at the top of the steep, winding, stone street that leads from the old government center to lower Kiev. It is one of the oldest streets in Kiev and is now a major tourist attraction with vendors selling traditional Ukrainian folk art, paintings, and Soviet memorabilia. We had walked down the street the year before with Yaroslav but had not bought anything. This time we bought a Ukrainian doll and a few hand carved boxes and boxes with inlaid straw decorations. It did wonders for our outlook and our relationship to get out of the apartment and have some fun.

When we got to the spot where Misha was supposed to pick us up, we discovered it had been turned into an impromptu market. People were selling things out of the backs of trucks and from little booths and tables. There was quite a variety for such a small market in the middle of the city, from cloth to nuts to live chicks and baby ducks to freshly dug raspberry plants and cherry trees. After we had toured the little market about three times, Misha finally found us and took us home.

Robert told Yuri he would like to go to the Catholic church on Sunday. The service stared at 11:00, so in the manner true to an Orthodox church member, Yuri said we would go at 11:30. I told him that Robert would probably want to be there at the beginning.

Yuri said, "It will go for an hour, right? We will go at 11:30 and that will be right in the middle of it."

We arrived at 11:30. The service was partly in Polish and partly in Ukrainian, which are very similar languages despite the fact that they use different alphabets. We found it very interesting and refreshingly familiar. They did not have kneelers though. When it was time to kneel, everyone knelt on the stone floor. At the end they had a little service honoring Mother Theresa, who had just died. Several people brought different objects symbolizing the things she had done and the ideals she stood for, placing them around Mother Theresa's picture in front of the altar. It was very touching, even though we did not understand the poem they read while they walked forward.

That service was a turning point for us. From that point on I held firm in my conviction that we would have the girls, no matter what anyone in Ukraine did. The Psalm response that week had been "Lord, let your mercy be upon us, as we place out trust in you." Even though we did not understand the language, the idea that God was still securely in charge and would be with us through the entire process came through and became a great part of our abiding faith.

After the service the weather had cleared, so Yuri took us to a pedestrian park along the Dnieper River, which still carries radioactive sediment from the Chernobyl accident upriver. We crossed a bridge to an island. It is a very popular and beautiful park with miles of trails, but we couldn't stay too long. We had to be back by at the apartment by 2:00 p.m. because Misha and Svetlana had to go to the airport to get the documents.

At the airport the plane finally landed and the package was on the plane, but the FedEx workers refused to give Svetlana the package. They just wanted to unload the plane and go home; not open the cartons to look for our package. Svetlana finally got a supervisor to come to the airport, make them open the boxes, and find our package. The FedEx employees were very put out with her, and I don't know what she had to promise them to get them to do it; no favor ever goes unpaid in the Ukrainian system. It took Misha and Svetlana until 9:00 to get the document. We went down to Svetlana's apartment when they got back. It was smaller than the apartment where we were staying but was very nicely furnished. Svetlana opened the package and checked the document. It was properly legalized and ready for approval by the Center for Adoptions.

Monday morning we were plagued by difficulties. We arrived at the Center for Adoptions by 9:15 a.m. to get their approval, but we had to wait about an hour and a half because they were having computer problems. Next we had to visit the notary's office to get legalization documents. After waiting for an hour or so there, Yuri, Robert, and I went in to find out what was taking so long.

"There is no one here who understands the computer program, so they don't know how to make the document," Yuri translated.

I looked at it and recognized that it was Word Perfect, but I couldn't understand the Russian keyboard or commands. Slowly, with Yuri translating the information on the screen, I managed to help the secretary prepare about half the document before the regular computer operator showed up. She produced the necessary document in a couple of minutes.

We bought gasoline at a little station on the way to Kirovograd. Soon the car stopped, and Misha couldn't get it started again. Seemingly there was water in the gasoline. Some men stopped to help and finally got the car started, but it kept sputtering and choking the rest of the way. We didn't get to Kirovograd until 4:30 p.m. Lana was waiting for us when we arrived and said that she had made everyone promise to stay at City Hall until 4:00 p.m. waiting for us. It is common for people to leave early if nothing is going on. The orphanage inspector had waited, but the person who could have put our case on the City Council agenda for the following Wednesday had already left, so we were not sure if our case would be heard by the City Council that week or if we would have to wait until the second Wednesday in November. We decided that if we were going to have to wait three more weeks for the City Council to hear the case Robert would go home and I would stay in Kirovograd. Lana reassured us that she had influence enough to make things go well in court if we could get the adoption through the city council.

Lana, Sergei, and Anna had moved into the new apartment they had been fixing up when we were there in 1996. It was in one of the better parts of town and close to a hospital, which meant that the electricity and water there went off occasionally but not too often. At one point Robert said he would have bought the apartment next door, knocked the wall out and had a five-room apartment. They couldn't figure out why a family of three should need anything more than a two-room apartment.

Tuesday morning we were assured that the Orphan's Council would meet and consider the documents that afternoon, but Svetlana was told that the City Council had met on Monday. After a hurried and agitated conver-sation with Svetlana, Lana went rushing down to City Hall to find out what was going on. She was told that the City Council had not met but would meet as scheduled the next Wednesday.

We realized that although Svetlana knew how to complete an adoption in Kiev, things were very different in Kirovograd. In Kirovograd we had to rely on Lana to know what was going on and she was able to help us more. We also had a much more open relationship with Lana because of our friendship. We could confide in Lana, and she would explain more than Svetlana thought was appropriate about what was going on.

Chapter 18

Where you go, I will go, where you stop, I will stop. Your people will be my people and your God my God. Ruth 1:26

"They came back. They said they would. My Papa came back," Anastasia kept repeating to Snijana.

"But where are they now?" asked Snijana. "They came twice, but now they are gone again."

"But they came back for us. If they came back once, they will come again," Anastasia insisted.

Irina watched and listened. She knew something big was up. Her sisters were really excited. She just wanted to be warm and cozy again, and she wished the lady would come back. She had never felt like that before in her life.

Pavlik came in as the argument ended and said, "I am going to Germany for surgery. The Canadians arranged it. After the surgery I will be able to go to the bathroom like other boys."

"That is great," said Anastasia. She was glad Pavlik was getting the surgery, but she was also afraid that after the surgery he would be sent to the other orphanage and she would never see him again. How could they get married if they lost track of each other?

"When my Papa comes back, I will ask him if he can find a home for you in America, too, so we will still be able to get married," promised Anastasia.

They kissed each other good-bye, and Pavlik left with Luba.

Mama and Papa did come back. One day after naptime Natasha told the girls to get dressed quickly because their Mama and Papa would be there soon. Anastasia shot a triumphant glance at Snijana before running off to get her hair braided by Natasha.

When Mama and Papa came with Lana, they had a suitcase with them.

"Are we leaving now?" asked Anastasia.

"No, but we are going to have fun today," promised Lana.

Mama and Papa opened the suitcase and brought out about thirty pairs of shoes. Sveta started looking at all the shoes, discussing with Lana which would be good for the children and which were too heavy or unsuitable in some other way. Snijana pushed herself between Sveta and Lana and watched as they sorted the shoes. Anastasia played with her Papa.

After Sveta, Lana, and Mama had sorted the shoes, they pulled some clothes out of the suitcase. Mama handed Anastasia some clothes, which she began to change into right away.

"I told you we were going home," she told Snijana.

"We are not going home today; we are just going to get some pictures taken," replied Lana as she was dressing Irina.

Snijana watched as Mama pulled a green corduroy romper out of the suitcase. She fell in love with it immediately. She tried to pull on the romper but had never worn anything like it before. It had snaps all over the place, and she wasn't sure which snaps she should unsnap and which she could leave snapped. Mama helped her put it on so that all the snaps and all the straps were right. She did like it when Mama helped her, but she wasn't going to get her hopes up just yet. Snijana would be happy to stay here if she could just have some new clothes to wear. She had decided to be happy with whatever she had. Anastasia wanted more things and more attention, but Snijana would be different.

After all three girls were dressed to Mama's satisfaction, their hair combed and faces washed, Mama picked up Irina, Papa took Anastasia's hand, and Lana took Snijana's hand. They walked out of the room and to the stairs. Snijana got scared. She didn't like going down the big concrete steps because she had fallen once and was afraid she might fall again. She slowly started down, holding onto Lana's hand with one hand and the railing with the other. Papa stopped and turned around. He picked Snijana up and carried her down the steps. She could tell that this did not make Anastasia happy, but for once she didn't care. This might be okay after all, if Papa would keep taking care of her when she was scared.

Misha and Svetlana waited for them in a car in the driveway. As they approached the car, Irina realized they were going to get into it. The big machine terrified her. She had seen cars take kids away, and they never came back. They would not get her into a car. She grabbed the doorframe and held on. After struggling for a while Mama handed Irina to Svetlana and got into the car. For a minute Irina thought she had won. They were not taking her away. But then Svetlana tried to hand her to Mama. She grabbed the doorframe again held on with all her might. Mama, Svetlana, and Lana pried her hands off and pushed her into the car. Her terrified screams continued while Mama held her tight. She finally calmed down a little when Anastasia got into the car and told her to hush.

Anastasia was really happy. "See, we are going with them," she told Snijana.

When the car started, Irina got scared all over again. She started screaming again and tried to climb out the back window. Papa had to help hold Irina so she wouldn't hurt Mama or anybody else, so Anastasia turned her attention to Misha, the nice man who was driving the car.

"Why do they have those lights?" she asked, pointing outside the car to the colored lights on poles.

"The red light means stop; the green light means go."

Anastasia watched the traffic lights and told him to stop when it was red and go when it was green. When Snijana saw what Anastasia was doing, she stood up and leaned over the seat. Soon both of them were yelling *zipiniti* for the red lights and *iti* for the green.

They parked downtown. Papa lifted Anastasia off his lap onto the sidewalk. Nobody else was getting out of the car. Maybe they were going to abandon her here. She tried to climb back in. Papa pushed on her. By now Svetlana was out of the car, and she held Anastasia until Papa got out and took her hand. She hadn't known they would all get out. They walked to a little shop where Misha told them to sit in chairs and wait while Svetlana talked to the man in the shop. Anastasia sat next to Misha.

"What are we doing here?" she asked.

"You are getting passport pictures taken so when you are ready to leave all the papers will be ready," he told her.

"Then after we leave here we will go home with Mama and Papa?" she asked.

"No. You will have to go back to the orphanage," he said.

That made her mad and disappointed at the same time. She had been so sure they were going home. Svetlana told her it was time to get her picture taken, but she refused to go.

Snijana had been watching and listening, and she thought it would be great fun to sit on the tall stool and get her picture taken. When Anastasia refused, Svetlana asked if Snijana would like to go first. She climbed up on the stool, which wobbled a little and was scary, but she was really brave and got her picture taken. When she finished, Misha gave her some chewing gum and told Anastasia she could have some too, if she would get her picture taken. Anastasia climbed up on the stool and smiled for the camera. Snijana knew Anastasia really wanted some gum and would do just about anything to get it.

Then it was Irina's turn. She had stopped crying, but was really sleepy now, and had just snuggled into Mama's shoulder when they tried to get her to sit on the stool. She sat looking down and pouting. Svetlana held up a pretty stuffed toy and called to her, but she refused to look at it. Anastasia waved her arms and told her to look at the camera, but she refused to move. Everyone tried to get her to lift her head, but she would not do it. She tried to slip off the stool when they talked to her. Finally, the cameraman was getting frustrated, so Mama knelt in front of Irina and held her on the stool while Svetlana lifted her head and held it in the right position as the cameraman snapped the picture. After three tries they got a picture that would meet the requirements for passport documents.

When Anastasia realized that they really were going back to the orphanage, she was very angry and refused to have anything to do with Papa for the rest of the day.

Pavlik finally came back; he didn't feel much like playing.

"The airplane ride to Germany took a long time," he said. "Then they took me to the hospital and put me in a big bed that was like a cage. The surgery was the second day."

"What does surgery mean?" asked Anastasia.

"It means they cut you with a knife and sew things back together so they are right," he told Anastasia.

"Did it hurt?"

"They made me sleep when they did the surgery, but it hurt afterward. The nurses gave me lots of medicine so I wouldn't get an infection. The doctors said infection is common."

"What is infection?"

"I don't know, but I think it is pretty bad. They really didn't want me to get an infection."

Anastasia sat quietly on a bench with him while they talked. She realized she had not asked Papa to find him a place to live in America.

When Papa showed up the next day she ran right to him and asked if they could take Pavlik, too. Lana talked with Papa a little bit, then said they would try to find a home for Pavlik. That made Anastasia feel better. She felt really bad that she had forgotten about it while he was gone.

Chapter 19

I can do all things through Christ who strengthens me. Philippians 4:13

Sue called that weekend and we told her about Pavlik and his need for ongoing medical care that wasn't available in Ukraine. She said they had an application from a single man, a doctor, who might be an excellent father for Pavlik They would start working on that as soon as they had completed our adoption.

We calculated how much longer we would be in Ukraine. We wanted to be conservative, so we calculated an extra day for everything. On Wednesday we would fax the City Council approval to the Center for Adoptions in Kiev, then send the original document by bus. They would return a document that told the judge that we could adopt the girls. Then the judge would hold a hearing. That could take three days. We would need to get a couple more papers in Kirovograd, so we allowed a day for that. Then there would be one day for a big party at the orphanage, and we would be off to Kiev. It would take about three days in Kiev to get the paperwork taken care of at the Ministry of Education and the State Department; then we would fly to Warsaw. One day for medical exams and one day for the visas there, and we figured we would be home by the first week in November.

After we had the passport pictures taken, we couldn't take the girls out of the orphanage, and we didn't see Luba very much. Pavlik was in need of much attention, and she was getting many repairs made on the orphanage. Also, she did not want to be accused of taking bribes or being unduly influenced by us.

Svetlana attended the meeting of the Orphan's Council. Svetlana and

Lana said it was pointless for us to attend because we would just have to sit in the hallway. So we waited at Lana's house. They approved the adoption! The next step was the City Council Approval, and they were scheduled to meet the following Wednesday. Svetlana returned to Kiev, and we stayed in Kirovograd.

Lana planned to speak at a German conference about alternative education that summer, and she wanted a video of her class for that presentation. Robert agreed to film it for her, so we spent several mornings in her classroom videotaping her. Sometimes I helped her students with their work. Since Lana's class used an American Christian curriculum and learned English, most of the students could understand what I was saying if I spoke slowly enough, but some of them were better than others.

One day Lana asked Anna and a boy from the class to take us to City Hall to deliver some papers. They were the best English speakers and loved the time out of school. On the way back to class we stopped and bought them some flowers for helping. The boy was very embarrassed to be given a rose for helping us because roses symbolize love to Ukrainians. We told him to give it to his mother.

Many Ukrainians still eat with only a spoon and what we consider a paring knife. In many places, forks are considered an instrument of the devil, so they don't use them. Lana told us that she had bought forks and table knives and learned to use them herself, because she never knew what social situations she might get into as a teacher. We attended a tea that Lana had arranged to teach the children proper table manners and the use of a fork.

The students, especially some of the boys, were not too interested in learning proper table manners. They stood up during the tea, and when Lana told them to sit back down, they leapt over the backs of their chairs shouting something that I think was the Ukrainian version of "Geronimo!" This tea was practice for a meal the students would have at a restaurant owned by the grandparents of one student, and I hoped they were quieter and better behaved at the restaurant.

Over the weekend, Sergei drove us to visit Sophia Park. Although all of the parks we visited in Ukraine were beautiful, this was the most impressive. It was built two hundred years ago by Polish prince for his Greek bride Sophia as a private park around their mansion. During the construction of the park, many peasants lost their lives or were crippled as rocks fell on them. Some were buried in landslides as they worked by hand to reshape the land into elaborate pathways, manmade hills, lakes, fountains, stonework, and meticulously designed plants. Sophia Park later belonged to the Russian Royal family, who made improvements in the fountains and waterworks and added more varieties of plants. The park was very well maintained in contrast with most of the city infrastructure. We hired a guide, who took us around the park, explaining how the hills had been formed out of the flat plains of Central Ukraine to resemble the Greek Sophia's homeland. Twenty-foot boulders had been hauled in and placed by hand. The ponds had been dug by hand, and the spectacular fountains and streams were gravity fed.

Although they had created a Greek landscape they had not been able to change the climate. A biting wind swept across the steppes that day, and even with our warmest clothes we were freezing before the tour had gone very far. We did not see the entire park because it was just too cold to stay out in the wind that long. Our guide told us that spring is the prettiest time to visit, and we vowed to come back sometime in spring to see the flowering trees.

Although Lana tried to plan activities for us, many of our days were spent sitting in her apartment waiting until we could go see the girls. We would get up around 8:30, spend some time journaling and reading our devotionals, which kept us centered on God, eat breakfast, then play solitaire or watch movies until it was time to go. We were permitted to see the girls in the morning before their lunch or in late afternoon after their nap. The instructors had asked us not to come during their music time because they were practicing a very important program. Robert and I had plenty of time to talk, but we didn't. He tends to become very quiet when he is emotionally stressed. I tried to talk with him and got no response. Fortunately Lana was there. She and I talked while she prepared meals, while we cleaned up, while we walked, and while we sat in the kitchen drinking tea.

But while Lana was at school, we had only the cards and the television. Ukrainian television stations get their programming from all over the world. They do not use subtitles; rather they dub in Russian or Ukrainian words over the original language. The original English, French, German, or Spanish can be heard at very low volume under the Russian or Ukrainian. I got to the point that I could tell the original language by "reading" the lips of the actors. Each language involves unique positioning of the mouth. The actor's lips would pucker in a certain way if it was French. If the language was Spanish, the lips were full and open. German speakers had more flattened mouths. I could usually tell if the actors were speaking English by listening but could not understand all of the dialog because the language dubbed over was so much louder.

Lana had a few movies in English without any dubbing. Several of these were children's movies she used at her school. We soon tired of watching these. Because of the difficulty in understanding the television, we preferred to play solitaire. We had to share one pack of cards, so Robert hovered over me until I finished a game, and I did the same with him. Lana had given us a little electric heater for our room because it was colder than the other room. We sat in front of the heater and played solitaire by the hour. When Robert was growing up, playing cards was his family's favorite Saturday night activity, but for some reason he and I almost never played any card games together during the time we were in Ukraine. Anna and I occasionally played War and they tried to teach us a traditional Ukrainian card game, but we never learned it well enough to be competitive. Lana finally bought a deck of cards, and she and Anna learned to play Solitaire, too.

We kept the heater going most of the time, even after the central heat came on. In Kirovograd it came on October 20. Lana assured us that our thirty dollars a day was paying for the food, electricity, and everything else we were using, even though electricity cost a lot. Because of phone calls to Kiev and the United States, the phone bill was soon more than one hundred dollars. At that point, someone from the telephone company came to the door to collect. Lana paid it with the money we had given her, and the woman who had come to collect was very pleased to get the money immediately. Most Ukrainians officially earned twenty to one hundred dollars a month. We figured it cost about five dollars a day to feed us, although we were eating better than average Ukrainians. We never found out exactly what the apartment and utilities cost, but with our American extravagance, we probably used more than twenty dollars worth of electricity a month, a huge amount by Ukrainian standards.

Sergei held the second largest amount of stock in his business, and he and Lana were doing well despite the government and Mafia interference. Lana told us that if a business paid all the taxes that they were supposed to it totaled about 120 percent of their income. Many Ukrainians still had the Soviet mindset and struggled with the fact that life as they knew it had completely disappeared. The entire country suffered from post-traumatic stress syndrome. This isn't the first time it happened to the Ukrainians. The wars of Europe and Asia had devastated Ukraine throughout most of it's history.

Svetlana came back to Kirovograd the following Tuesday and found out that the City Council had met the day before and had not considered the adoption. We were all furious that we had not been notified about the meeting so we could get our case on the agenda. Lana made several phone calls and got a special meeting arranged for Thursday afternoon.

In the meantime the Orphanage Inspector found several discrepancies in the paperwork that would need to be corrected. Luba was from Belarus and had spelled Snijana the Russian way. It had also been spelled the Russian way in the original documents removing them from their mother's custody, because Russian was still the official language in Ukraine at the time. All the other papers spelled it the Ukrainian way. On Wednesday Svetlana and her driver took the orphanage inspector to Alexandria, about one hundred kilometers away, to meet with the judge who had made the original separation papers. They also had to see Luba to get the spelling corrected and to get written certification that it was the same girl whether her name was spelled the Russian or the Ukrainian way.

We spent Wednesday afternoon working on the video at the school, then went to the orphanage to take pictures of the girls. The camera got jammed just as we started taping them. This annoyed Robert who spent the rest of Wednesday trying to get it fixed. He couldn't, so he gave it to Sergei to see if he could find someone to fix it. We never found anyone in Ukraine who could fix the camera, so we didn't have any videos of our time there.

Thursday was October 30, and Yaroslav invited us to a Halloween party his students had prepared at the University in Kirovograd where he was teaching the Senior English class. We first talked with two first-year classes and gave some of the students their first experience with American English. Then we went to the Halloween party. Halloween is not generally celebrated in Ukraine, so everything researched Halloween through books and movies. Many of the costumes were excellent. Yaroslav had divided the students into groups to write and act out Halloween skits. Most of the skits were really bad. Then they bobbed for apples. The students convinced Yaroslav to try, and he got an apple.

At the University we also met Oksana, who agreed to take us shopping and to be our interpreter when we went to the orphanage. With another interpreter Lana could spend more time at school and leave only to take care of official business. Okasana, besides being one of the most beautiful girls I have ever seen, had spent time in England, was completely fluent in English, and was happy to show us around her hometown.

After we left the university, we went to School # 11 to send an e-mail to friends back in the United States. We had noticed that Lana seemed to be in trouble at the school for missing so much work, and we could see that her relationship was strained with some of the other teachers while we were there. We were sorry for jeopardizing her job, but she did not seem to find it important.

At 3:30 p.m. Lana and Svetlana sent us home while they went to the City Council meeting. They still weren't home by dinnertime, so I fixed dinner for Robert, Anna and myself; then we watched television, waiting for them to come back. Sergei had also joined them at the courthouse after work. We waited and waited then finally went to bed. At 11:30 p.m. Lana and Sergei came home. She immediately made several phone calls, then explained what had happened.

The City Council approved the adoption, but the mayor had at first refused to sign the documents. They spent several hours persuading him before they convinced the mayor to sign. At Sergei's office they faxed the signed approval to Kiev then went to the train station to put it on the train. The train for Kiev had already left, so they drove to another city fifty kilometers away. They arrived ahead of the train and managed to get the documents on board. Misha would pick the documents up in Kiev at 5:00 in the morning and take them to the Center for Adoptions. The Center for Adoptions would then approve the adoption, and we could apply for a court date to finalize the adoption. The Center for Adoptions would rush their approval through and fax the document back. Because of the delay by the City Council, the timetable had slipped a little. We were now assuming we would be home with the girls between November 10 and 14.

Chapter 20

Forgetting what is behind and straining toward what is ahead I press on toward the goal to win the prize for which God has called me heavenward in Christ Jesus. Philippians 3:13-14

"What names have you chosen for the girls?" Lana asked.

We sat in the office of the Orphanage Inspector, writing out the application to adopt the girls to be presented to the judge. The Orphanage Inspector told Lana what the application had to include, Lana asked us questions, then translated back into Ukrainian. Then the Orphanage Inspector wrote the answers. The application had to say that we wanted to adopt three girls and state their new names.

"Anastasia Marie Habiger-Doxon, Janalyn Suzanne Habiger-Doxon and Lydia Irene Habiger-Doxon."

The inspector wanted to know why they had two surnames and two given names.

"It is a tradition in America," I told her.

"What is their patronym?" she asked. A patronym is the father's name with a suffix *ovna* for girls, *vich* for boys.

"Americans didn't have patronyms," we explained. "But you could put 'Robertovna' if you want to."

Lana and the Inspector decided to defer that question and go on to nationality.

"American," I said.

"No. They can't be American. They might someday have American citizenship but that is not their nationality."

I asked, "Aren't they Ukrainian?"

"Their father was Russian. Their mother was Ukrainian," the Inspector told us. "It is more common to list the father's nationality than the mother's, but you can have them be any nationality you want."

"Except American," I said. They looked at me like I was just trying to be difficult.

"They should be the nationality of the parents," Lana interpreted.

"I am German, Russian, English, and Dutch, and Robert is Slovakian, German, and Irish"

That made it worse because in Ukraine a person is only supposed to have one nationality. Finally they wrote a statement that it is not the tradition in America to list patronym or nationality so that was not necessary. Next they asked for birth dates and birthplace.

"Can we just have any birth date that we want?" I asked.

"Yes," they said. "Is there a special day you would like to have as their birthday? It is quite common to change the birth dates because children are generally a little delayed developmentally when they have been in the orphanage. Having a later birth date would give them more of a chance to catch up."

We decided to leave their birth dates and birthplace the same. The orphanage inspector wrote a little more about us wanting to adopt the girls, Lana proofread it and copied it over in her schoolteacher's penmanship, we signed where she told us to sign and then went to get it notarized. The whole process took about an hour and a half.

A lawyer Lana knew had said that we could take all our paperwork to the

The picture the started it all!
At Orphanage June, 1995

Lynn waiting in front of the Orphanage.

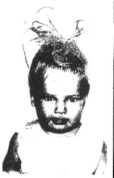

Lydia, Age 2
Faxed photo

Janalyn, Age 2

Anastasia, Age 3

The day we returned to the Orphanage, October, 1997.
(Anastasia, Robert, Janalyn, Lynn, Lydia)

Anastasia and Lynn dancing.

Janalyn, passport photo

Lynn feeding a
banana to Lydia.

Pavlik and Anastasia

Anastasia with Lydia

Janalyn as a fox

Robert with Lydia
drawing pictures

Janalyn learning to read

Embroidery on back of pageant costumes.

The girls ready for a program.

Anastasia, boy, and Janalyn

Anastasia, Yuri, and Janalyn
in penguin costumes.

Orphanage Director

Caregivers and children

Lydia
Anastasia
Christmas 1997
Janalyn

Going away party at Orphanage
One of three cakes

First Bath!

Svetlana: ICA Coordinator   Lana   Sergi with Anastasia
And her husband Misha

Anna: Daughter of Lana and Sergi   Lynn with Lana's Parents

Lyudmilla: Assistant   Oxana: Interpreter in   Yuri: Interpreter
Director International   Kirovograd   in Kiev
Center for Adoption

Kiev looking south from Monastery bell tower.

At Kiev Park: Yaroslav, Robert, Julia
Lynn, Anya, and Rich Castle

Robert and Lynn at
Entrance to Monastery

Apartment in Kirovograd

Girls and Lynn at Dallas airport
waiting for INS.

Anastasia, Lynn, and Lydia
first off the airplane.

Ed Slater with Lydia at airport.

Anastasia, Robert, and Janalyn

Friends greeting us at airport homecoming.

Grandma Lydia, a tired
Lydia and Lynn

judge as soon as we had written the statement, but the Inspector would not release the documents. She may have thought we would make changes in them while we had them in our possession. Lana and Svetlana took us home and went to the lawyer's office to see what they could do about getting the document released and taken to the judge. We were to be on standby in case they got the papers. They were also waiting for the Center for Adoptions to fax their approval. The Orphanage Inspector said she would bring the papers to the judge when we had the fax from Kiev. We waited the rest of the day for the fax. It arrived half an hour after the judge had gone home, even though he had waited an extra hour to receive the papers. We now had to wait until Monday to take the papers to the judge. The hearing should be a mere formality now that we had all the approvals.

That first weekend in November we once again planned the trip home, dreaming of a warm bathroom and drinking water straight from the tap. A pile of work waited for us, after a month away, but we tried not to think about that. We had kept in touch by e-mail and telephone, so we had some idea of how things were going at the office. Our church clients were still very supportive of our continued absence. Maria and Katrina, our architectural intern, who had grown up in their parents' businesses, were managing the business very well. Ken, the only other registered architect on the staff, had doubled his workload to see that projects were completed on time.

We also planned the trip to Warsaw, where the Embassy issued U.S. visas for the entire region. There is only a consulate in Kiev, not an Embassy. Robert was very excited about going to Warsaw. He really wanted to see the architecture and get a sense of the history of the city. All I thought only about dragging our luggage and the girls all over the city, trying to get a taxi in a language we didn't understand, changing money while trying not to lose track of three curious girls, and trying to find every office we needed in a strange city without anyone to help us. We were sure we would leave Ukraine by the end of the next week. Robert was scheduled to speak November 15 at a national conference on church architecture in Cincinnati, and he was very excited about the opportunity to present some of his ideas in that national forum.

In Ukraine there are municipal judges, district judges, and regional courts. Lana and Sergei knew the regional judge, but the hearing would be in the district court. On Monday morning we joined other petitioners in the crowded hallway outside the judge's office, arriving a little early for our 9:00 appointment. The Orphanage Inspector was not there with our file. Svetlana went to the Inspector's office to find her. The Inspector said she had to make copies of the documents. Fifteen minutes later, she came back and said the copy machine was broken and she would have to go to the office across the street to make the copies. Svetlana and the Inspector finally showed up at 9:30 a.m.

The judge's office opened off the center of the drab, dusty hallway in which we sat. Because we were Americans, we always got chairs. Once Robert offered his chair to an elderly woman who was waiting, but her sense of hospitality was so great that she insisted he sit in the chair. People were admitted one at a time in the order they arrived to talk with the judge. This was not the courtroom; most of the decisions were actually made in the judge's office. People waited in line in the hallway most of the day to see him, then had to plead, argue, beg, or bribe their way to a decision when they were admitted. If he did not want to make a decision, he ordered them to leave his office, and they would have to come back another day to stand in line again. While we sat in the hall, Lana spoke with other people there and learned that the judge could be quite erratic and subjective about giving his approval.

When Svetlana arrived, she went into the office to talk with his assistant. When she came out, she told us, "His assistant said we could wait, but he probably wouldn't be able to see us today." The Orphanage Inspector smiled when she said that.

Svetlana barged in when our turn came and talked with the judge; then she had the Inspector go downstairs and give the documents to a clerk. She made sure the clerk recorded receiving them on Monday, November 3.

"He is required by law to set a hearing date within thirty days," Svetlana said. "And the hearing has to be held within fifteen days of the date he sets."

Never before had Svetlana or ICA worked on such a difficult, time consuming, or expensive adoption in Ukraine. Two other couples were scheduled to arrive in Kiev to adopt other children, and Svetlana needed to be there. She tutored Lana in the way adoptions were supposed to happen, and Lana took on some of the duties of coordinator, on top of hostess and interpreter. Sue and Irina called every other day from Washington to see how things were going and how we were doing. Yet not once did anyone ask us to give up or to take other children from somewhere else. They understood that Anastasia, Snijana, and Irina were already our daughters, as decreed in heaven, and that we would prevail against the forces on earth that were trying to prevent the adoption.

After so many frustrating experiences, we had completely stopped accepting and going along with whatever we were told to do. Instead we demanded explanations of everything, which we sometimes got and sometimes did not. In spite of all the difficulties, we never again became as discouraged as we had been that first weekend when we had to go back to Kiev to get the medical forms corrected. We were determined to see the process through no matter what it took. We continued praying and believing that things could be worked out even when it seemed impossible.

After our time at the courthouse we went to the orphanage. There was one caregiver at the orphanage who seemed to resent the disruption to the routine whenever we came. Natasha frowned at us and seemed reluctant to let the girls play with us. We came to dread the times she was on duty when we showed up. She did not prevent us from playing with the girls, but when we took them outside, she would only let us have them outside for a little while, and she seemed to dislike having them out of her sight. She resented anything we did for the girls. We thought she was a very strict disciplinarian and did not like having the routine disrupted.

Lana had missed so much school that she had used up all her vacation time and sick leave. Monday afternoon she went to the doctor to get an excuse to be out of work for a while longer. She spent the rest of the afternoon calling people who might have influence with the judge. We were beginning to get worried that the hearing might not be as soon as we had hoped. In most of the other cases Svetlana had worked on the approvals by all the officials. Committees were the hardest part, and the judge's approval was more of a formality. For some reason, this judge wanted to have power over the process.

Tuesday morning, after waiting only about an hour and a half in the hallway, the assistant admitted us to the judge's office. It was freshly painted, carpeted, and clean. The judge sat behind a large, dark wooden desk and questioned us. He was much nicer to us than he had been to other foreign couples who had tried to adopt children. Lana told us that he had ignored some and had thrown others out of his office. As Lana and Svetlana had visited with others waiting in the hallway, they found out that the judge had managed to scare off anyone before us who had come to adopt children from this particular orphanage. This gave us even more resolve to see the process through. We were not going to give up on adopting these girls. We knew in our hearts that God meant these children for us.

After several minutes of discussion with Svetlana, the Judge agreed to hear the case, although he did not say when. It looked like he was going to delay as much as possible. He could also refuse to grant the adoption, but there was an appeal process. The appeal would be before the regional judge, who owed Sergei a favor.

Svetlana returned to Kiev for the four-day October Revolution holiday. After she left, we approached Lana.

"It is November. Why is the October Revolution celebrated in November?"

"It was October 25 by the old calendar, but it is November 7 by the new calendar."

"But communism has collapsed. There is no longer any need to celebrate the October Revolution."

"Everybody knows that, but they want a reason to celebrate anyway. Would you like to go downtown to participate in the demonstration on the town square?"

We declined.

Chapter 21

I waited patiently for the Lord and he turned to me and heard my cry.
Psalm 40:1

Mama and Papa came to play every afternoon. This was the best time of day for Snijana. Papa played horsie with her, and Mama gave her rides on her back. They also danced and sang with her. She tried to sing the songs with them, but the words were so funny she just couldn't say them fast enough. Snijana actually liked the picture books best.

After Pavlik returned from Germany, all Anastasia wanted to do was play Doctor every day. She took Papa's pen out of his pocket and pretended to give him a shot, then covered him with all the coats and scarves she could find. Sometimes she made Snijana play too, but mostly it was Anastasia's game with Papa. One day Papa brought her a little doctor kit. Then she started running around giving everyone shots and pretending to stick the thermometer up their bottoms. Snijana tried to stay as far away as she could when Anastasia was being a doctor. At least when Papa was there he kept Anastasia busy so Snijana didn't have to be the patient.

Irina still liked sitting on Mama's lap, but she would get off and play sometimes. She loved looking at the books Mama and Papa brought and drawing pictures. One of the books was about a big red dog named Clifford. Irina loved that one and Mama would read it to her over and over with those funny sounding words Snijana liked Irina to stay on Mama's lap, because when she got off she took books away from Snijana. If Snijana didn't give them up, Irina would hit her. This wasn't right. Irina was littler than she was. But Mama was really funny about it. She wouldn't let Snijana hit Irina back.

And when Anastasia hit Snijana, she got scolded, too, so Anastasia started hurting her only when Mama and Papa weren't looking.

What made Mama and Papa's visits really special was that Mama and Papa always brought food and little candy things. Anna said they were vitamins, not candy, but she didn't know what vitamins were. She liked the fruit they brought, especially the bananas. The first time they brought a banana Irina didn't know what it was. Mama had to force a piece into her mouth. The next time she was so eager to get to it that she bit Mama's finger as she was peeling it. Other times they brought tangerines or rolls of bread. Today when they came they brought something Anna called pizza. It had bread and cheese and a little meat.

One day Mama and Papa brought crayons and a whole book of blank paper for each of them to draw on. Snijana had never had so much fun in her entire life. She made big, colorful pictures on every page. Papa helped her and Anastasia make pictures of bananas, animals, birds, and trees. Even Ira got off of Mama's lap and handed her book to Papa to draw pictures.

Irina still didn't talk, but she understood that funny language Mama and Papa spoke. Mama said some funny sounding words, and Irina nodded and pointed. Mama held her up and let her look out the window a lot of times. When she stood on tiptoe, Snijana could see out the window any time she wanted, but she still wished Mama would hold her up to look out like she did Irina. Snijana kicked over the crayon box.

Mama put Irina down, frowned, and said some of those funny words to Snijana. Irina came over and picked up all the crayons. Mama smiled, pointed at Irina, and said some more funny words to Papa. Papa said some funny words to Irina, and she started to give Snijana's crayons to Mama. Snijana grabbed them back and went back to coloring.

After they left Snijana asked Anastasia, "Do those funny words Mama and Papa say mean anything?"

"I don't know," Anastasia said. "Natasha, do those funny words Mama says mean anything?"

"That is another language," Natasha said. "You know Russian and Ukrainian, but that language is called English. You will learn English when you go to America. Your Mama and Papa speak only English and do not understand Russian or Ukrainian."

Anastasia and Snijana had never met anyone who could only speak one language. Everyone they knew could speak both Russian, and Ukrainian and they had learned both languages before they were three. "If Papa can't understand me, I just won't talk," Anastasia said. She didn't say anything for three days.

Sveta planned a special program for their Mama and Papa, so Anastasia and Snijana had big parts in almost every song or skit. A program usually meant that the oldest kids would be moved out of the room. Snijana would be one of the oldest when Anastasia and the other kids her age left. Snijana liked that. She would miss Anastasia, but it would be fun being the oldest for once. One day she heard Natasha tell Lana that there were more than thirty babies in the hospital waiting for a place in the orphanage. New kids would be moved into their room, and maybe for once she would have somebody to boss around.

The day of the program they started getting ready right after breakfast. Sveta had gotten the traditional Ukrainian folk costumes out of the closet and ironed them, so that they would be pretty for the program. The girls put on the embroidered skirts and blouses, the boys the big pants and vests. All the girls had ribbons tied in their hair and everyone looked really beautiful, Snijana thought.

All the other kids in the orphanage except the babies came to the program. There were a few adults there, but not as many as had come to the May Day program. They sang traditional Ukrainian children's songs and recited some of the poetry they had memorized. Anastasia and Pavlik sang a love song as a duet. Irina did not perform in that program. She sat on Mama's lap through most of it. At the end of the program Anastasia and Snijana recited a poem saying that they loved their Mama and Papa and would obey them and do everything they were told to do. Then they thanked Mama and Papa for coming to get them. The staff then thanked Mama and Papa, and Mama and Papa thanked the staff for taking care of Snijana and her sisters for so long.

After the program, Papa had everyone stand up, and he took pictures of their costumes; then he had everyone turn around so he could take pictures of the embroidery on the back. They let Irina stand in line with the rest of them even though she did not have a costume on. She stood on tiptoe so she would look as tall as the others. When Papa took the pictures of the embroidery on the back, she turned around and looked at him. Snijana wished she would behave. She was ruining the picture. Papa wanted a picture from the back.

When the children went back to the room, Mama and Lana served bananas and little cakes for everyone. Snijana was so glad her Mama and Papa had brought food for everyone this time. Julia, that new little girl, kept trying to sit on Mama's lap. Irina started to cry when Julia climbed up beside her, and she tried to push Julia off. Finally Lana took Julia and held her for a while. Snijana was happy Lana had taken Julia. She just wanted her to stay away from her Mama.

Chapter 22

And now these three remain: faith, hope and love. But the greatest of these is love. I Corinthians 13:13

Sitting with the staff after the party, Lana told them, "The judge is refusing to hear the case."

"We will send a group to talk with him," said Sveta. "He has to say yes. This is the best thing that has happened around here in years."

"No. Don't go talk with him," Natasha said. "It will only get worse if you do."

"I don't think it would be wise to get involved," Luba said.

Lana tried every angle she knew to influence the judge. Every time we rode in a taxi she told the taxi driver we were trying to adopt three girls but the judge wouldn't set the date for the hearing. She said their children wouldn't have much of a chance when they grew up because all these orphans would be out on the street committing crimes or expecting to be supported by the government. We were trying to do everyone a favor and get at least some of them off the streets so their own children would have fewer problems to deal with, and yet the judge wouldn't even cooperate.

The judge had office hours three days a week, for three hours a day. On those days we sat in the hallway outside his office with everyone else who needed to see him. Sometimes as many as twenty people sat in that hallway. No one kept a list or sign-up sheet to record who arrived in what order, but everyone knew who was there before they came, and who arrived after, and everyone went into the office in the order they came. For some it just took a few minutes, others were in the office more than an hour. He never saw everyone who was waiting, and many came back again and again to try to get satisfaction. Because he was the lead judge in the district court, all people had to see him first to get their cases scheduled for a hearing or assigned to a lower ranked judge. He also made most of the decisions and told the other judges what to say in a hearing. We sat in the hall every day during his office hours, but only saw him three times in two weeks.

We came home furious after each meeting with him and sat with Lana to strategize the next step. Friction started to grow between ICA and Lana. Svetlana disapproved of Lana sharing so much information about what was going on with us. It had been her policy, as well as culturally correct behavior in Ukraine, to take care of everything and only share with the adoptive parents what they needed to know. Lana discussed everything with us and tried to work out a plan for the next meeting. There were a few things Lana did not tell us, but she talked rather openly with us. We preferred it that way. Svetlana and the ICA staff did not.

Lana could also act rashly and magnify problems. Svetlana was very careful and methodical, and although she got quite upset at times, she did not show it to either adoptive parents or officials if she could help it. Lana was the opposite. She got excited, and everyone knew it. Yet in Kirovograd, ICA could not get anything done. Svetlana and ICA had influential people from other regions in Ukraine call the judge, urging him to make a decision. Every time they did, he got even more obstinate and retracted promises he had made previously.

Soon people all over the district were hearing about our attempts to adopt the girls. A newspaper reporter interviewed us and took pictures of us with the girls in the orphanage. My picture holding Irina was on the front page of the local newspaper. Mr. Malyuta called the judge and asked him to make a favorable decision and was rebuffed. Margarita, the principal of School # 11, called and asked the judge to make a favorable decision.

One evening we were invited to dinner at the house of a local architect, who had a son in Lana's class. We had a great time visiting with him. He and Robert debated the merits of Soviet versus American architecture. We discovered that his wife was the godmother to a child whose godfather was the judge. She agreed to call him and talked with him more than once, asking for a favorable decision.

On another evening Oksana invited us to her house. We were to go on our own, so Lana carefully instructed us on the proper gifts to take and told us, "Make sure you take your shoes off right away when you go into the house, talk with her grandmother more than anyone else, and eat whatever they feed you." We felt a little like one of her elementary students, but to be honest we did sometimes forget to take our shoes off in Ukrainian houses and probably would not have talked much with Oksana's grandmother.

Oksana's father was a prominent surgeon in town, and he was interested in finding out more about our difficulties with the adoption. Her family lived on the second floor of a pre-Soviet home. It was much more spacious and ornate than the Soviet-style apartments. Oksana's grandmother grilled us about our intentions and the reasons we did not have children of our own. Okasana's father had caught a fish, which was deliciously prepared for our meal and Oksana and two of her friends entertained us with excellent piano music. We thoroughly enjoyed our evening. Oksana's father called the judge and asked him to make a favorable decision. Surely the judge could not figure out how these strange Americans could have so many friends in so many walks of life who wanted them to adopt these girls.

Lana's father had been a driver and her mother a cook and housekeeper, who now sold sunflower seeds in the market, so Lana was well connected with the underground network of gossip that circulated in the city. She was also connected with the intellectuals at the university, the business people Sergei worked with, and the wealthy parents of her students. Because she was so outgoing and quick to observe new customs, she could fit into all these groups. Through her many conversations we discovered that the judge had political ambitions and didn't want to deal with foreign adoptions. He decided that granting a foreign adoption would make some people angry and refusing to grant it would make others unhappy, and he did not want to alienate anyone. Yet all these prominent people kept calling him. He was getting more antagonistic as we refused to just give up and go away.

Time was working against us. Robert was not going to make it back to do the presentation in Cincinnati. He called his office in Albuquerque and sent Ken, the senior staff member to make the presentation he had prepared. Robert was becoming very angry and bitter. Even with a very competent staff more problems were cropping up. Robert really needed to be there to make decisions, to complete designs, and to interview for new projects. It was becoming clear that he needed to be home.

Robert made plans to go home on November 16 unless the judge had set the court date by then. I would stay with Lana and keep working to get the judge to set the date. I felt depressed and angry by this time, but I vowed I would not go home without the girls

We got in to see the judge twice in the next week. The first time he told us that we would need a lawyer. He gave us a list of lawyers he recommended. We immediately decided not to use a lawyer who was probably in cahoots with the judge. The lawyer Lana knew told her that she would take the case for seven thousand dollars. Svetlana disagreed. None of the other cases she had ever worked with had needed a lawyer. We had all the other approvals we needed, and the judge's ruling was just supposed to be a formality. She said she would take care of it without a lawyer.

After another visit to the judge, Svetlana also decided we needed a lawyer. Valerie, the lawyer for Sergei's business, agreed to work with us. Every lawyer in Ukraine had a ranking or position in the legal system. We were not sure if this was an official or unofficial ranking. Lana said our lawyer outranked the judge but had spent time in prison during communist times because he refused to reveal some confidential information he had gotten from former clients. He was also a born-again Christian and had endured persecution during Communist times. He agreed to take the case for one hundred dollars. We gave him the money and he went to see the judge. When he came back, he told us that it would be difficult but he knew what to do. We were incredibly angry by this time that the judge would not hear the case. We were spending more money every day, as well as losing money from Robert's business and not doing anything constructive. Our frustration and anger built up, and we had nobody but each other to express it to, for fear of upsetting the people who were helping us. As a result we got more depressed and did not communicate much with each other, except late at night lying in bed. One night Lana told us Sergei had heard us talking in the middle of the night and was worried that we were feeling bad. After that we didn't even discuss things in the middle of the night.

Except when we played with the girls, I had almost forgotten how to smile. On the streets, I was often mistaken for a Ukrainian. I was wearing Lana's warm clothes, but also my expression had become the serious, determined expression of the Ukrainians as they struggled to survive in a broken down economy with their homes, streets, and society deteriorating all around them. Svetlana would take Robert back to Kiev on Friday, November 16 to catch his flight home. Although they were all praying for the process, even our most patient and understanding clients were becoming less patient and understanding. Our business was losing money because Robert was not there, and we couldn't afford to lose any more.

The night before Robert left, Lana was on the phone for a long time with Svetlana, then Sue. When she hung up, she told me everyone agreed that I should go home, too. There was nothing I could do there. Lana and the lawyer could take care of everything. I had vowed I would not leave Ukraine again without the girls, but they didn't give me any options. I cried all night. Until then I had been healthy despite the fact that almost everyone around me had coughs, colds or some other problem. As soon as they told me I had to go home, I felt my throat starting to get sore. By morning I had a serious cough. The next morning, I packed a few things to take home, leaving most of our things there, and we went to the orphanage to say good-bye to the girls.

Chapter 23

Now faith is being sure of what we hope for and certain of what we do not see.
Hebrews 11:1

Anastasia could tell that there was something wrong when Mama and Papa and Lana came to see them. Usually Mama and Papa were really happy. They smiled more than anyone else she knew, especially Mama. But today Mama was not smiling at all. She was also coughing a lot. They hadn't brought the doctor kit, so Anastasia got Papa's pen and pretended to give Mama a shot. Maybe even a pretend shot would make her feel better.

Lana said Mama and Papa had to go home to get the house ready. She told them they would have Grandma bake a cake for the girls, so it would be ready when they got there.

Anastasia looked at Mama and Papa with disbelief. They had said they were there to take her home this time. She started to cry. Mama squeezed Irina so tight Irina wiggled off her lap.

Lana said, "They will just be gone for a little while." Anastasia remembered the last time Mama and Papa had gone away "for a little while."

"Do you want to have a cake?" Lana asked. "They have to go home to get Grandma to bake a cake. You wouldn't want to go there and not have anything good to eat, would you?"

Anastasia shook her head.

"I will come and see you while they are gone," Lana promised. "And I will bring you more pizza."

Anastasia stopped crying. After all, wasn't it Lana who always talked with her, who laughed at her jokes. And it was Lana who made the pizzas, too. Lana wasn't leaving.

"Big girls like you shouldn't cry," Lana said. "Besides, they won't bring you pretty things if you look so angry. If you cheer up, your Mama and Papa will bring you lots of beautiful things from America."

Anastasia smiled. Sveta had been telling her about America. It sounded like a really wonderful place. They had lots to eat there; everyone lived in big houses and drove nice cars. Papas worked in big tall office buildings and wore fancy clothes. Natasha let her watch *Dallas* on TV. She said that Dallas was in America. Anastasia was looking forward to going to America, and if she was going to have a grandma like Ellie on *Dallas* that would be wonderful. If they had to go get their big, beautiful house ready, she supposed that would be okay She gave Mama and Papa the thumbs up.

"See, I told you," said Snijana. "They really are never going to take us with them."

"They are, too, and we will live on a ranch like in *Dallas*. We will have horses and a big house and lots of cars. Papa will work in a big office, and we will be able to buy anything we want."

Snijana just walked away. Anastasia was beginning to not believe it herself.

Chapter 24

You need to persevere so that when you have done the will of God, you will receive what He has promised. Hebrews 10:36

I managed to not cry until we were walking out of the orphanage. By the time we got to the car, Lana was crying, too. She promised she would do whatever it took to make the girls ours. The tears ran down my face all the way to Kiev.

In Kiev Svetlana sent us to the drug store with Yuri to buy something for my cough. In Ukraine people can buy any kind of medicine without a prescription, provided they have enough money. The main problem the pharmacist had was that I am allergic to penicillin, so he had to give me another antibiotic. It did not seem to do much good. Our hostess gave me a drink made from viburnum berries and that seemed to calm the cough better than anything else I tried.

Robert had already gotten his ticket with frequent flyer miles through the travel agent in Washington, but no one in Kiev could issue a frequent flyer ticket, so we had to buy a one-way ticket for me to London. Once we arrived in London, we got my ticket home and back to Kiev with Robert's frequent flyer miles. We were in England for about twenty hours but just went to the hotel, turned on the television to hear English coming out of it, ate a meal that did not contain sausage, pickles or fried potatoes, then went to sleep. We emerged the next day at the Albuquerque airport tired, defeated, and extremely depressed. I don't even remember the first week home.

On Sunday, the pastor asked us to speak about our experience. Until I started preparing to tell the church about what had happened in Ukraine, I did not realize how much I needed this break and this chance to rest and recover from the struggle there. We asked people to keep praying that the judge would set the date quickly so we could have the girls home by Christmas. That became our mantra: "Have the girls home by Christmas."

Lana had said that of all the things we had in America, the thing she envied the most was our church community. Within the church we could speak openly about anything, and people supported us through the best of times and the worst of times. We realized the importance of that community as they supported and encouraged us as we waited. Prayer, more than anything else, was making this adoption happen.

Robert returned to his normal schedule, trying to catch up with as much work as possible and get things in order so he would be prepared to return to Ukraine. The doctor said my cough was caused by a virus and there wasn't much she could do. I wished I had some of that viburnum berry tea the Ukrainians used. I worked half days and spent most of the rest of the day in bed.

Because it had taken so long and cost so much to pay translators, drivers, and other costs all the money we had sent to ICA and taken to Ukraine was gone. We needed to take eleven thousand dollars on our next trip to Ukraine. The business had been so neglected that we did not have any way to get that sort of money. Robert was explaining this to Bob Prindle, whom we had selected as Janalyn's godfather, and he offered to make us a short-term loan of ten thousand dollars.

During that time Robert was also able to go to Dodge City, Kansas, to interview for the design of a new Roman Catholic cathedral there. He received that contract, and it was to become our largest source of income for the next two years and the means by which we paid off the debts incurred through the adoption. God does promise that he will watch over and provide for those who do his will.

I refused to let any doubt about the outcome of the adoptions creep in. I bought Christmas dresses and some pretty matching slippers for the girls and immediately packed these into the suitcase we would take back. I collected gifts I knew would be appropriate for those who were helping, now that I knew them better. Because westerns are so popular in Ukraine, we bought a cowboy hat, bolo tie, and several Native American souvenirs. We got some silk scarves and other light but very lovely items. I also took a copy of the dramatized recording of *The Bible in Ukrainian* produced by Faith Comes by Hearing for Valerie. We had discovered that although Ukrainians often had difficulty meeting their most basic needs they considered gifts that were merely useful an insult. It implied that they were unable to take care of themselves. They appreciated luxury items, even though they were not really needed.

We celebrated Thanksgiving with Steve Herrera's family, still counting the days until the thirty-day limit for setting the court date so we could take some action. My birthday is December 2, which was also the twenty-ninth day after we had given the papers to the judge. On that day Sue, from ICA, called and said that the judge had finally set the court date. The news was the best birthday present I ever received. The judge had set the hearing December 8. We would leave on the 6th. That was great. We had four days to get ready this time. It seemed almost leisurely compared to our first trip.

When we arrived in Ukraine, the weather was colder than ever. Lana lent me her fur lined boots and heavy wool coat. I didn't own anything warm enough for a Ukrainian winter. We arrived in Kirovograd on December 7 and were in the hallway outside the judge's office at 8:30 on the December 8 even though the hearing was not scheduled until 10:30. As the judge walked in around 9:30, he was visibly shocked to see us. It was obvious that he thought by giving us four days to show up he had solved his problem. He didn't think we could make it back in time and he could just say that nobody showed up for the hearing. In fact, his assistant had already made an entry in the log that a hearing had been held but no one had been present. We did get in to see him, and he said he had expected us on November 27, and we had not been there. Everyone looked confused at that. Then he said he would not hold a hearing because some of the people who should be present were not there. We couldn't believe that he had scheduled a hearing and now he was refusing to have it. He told us he didn't want to see any more of us and we should get out. He told us to come back on Tuesday. We left confused and angry. How could he just refuse to hold a scheduled hearing?

Jesus had said, "Love your enemies," and the judge had gone from being just a difficult and obstinate man to being a true enemy. A battle between good and evil was being played out in front of us, and there was very little we could do but pray. We couldn't understand what was being said and didn't know the laws and customs of the country.

That afternoon we visited the girls. Natasha was on duty and talked to Lana for a while before she would let the girls play with us. She looked really angry and would only let us play with the girls for a little while. Snijana was happy to see us; she and Irina immediately began searching my bag to see what we had brought them. Anastasia was very angry with us for having left again, even though it had just been three weeks this time, not a year and a half. When Robert got some balloons out and blew them up, Anastasia got Pavlik, and the three of them batted the balloons around until she was laughing again; then she seemed to forgive us.

Lana was no longer working at the Christian school. She said it was mainly for health reasons, but we knew it had a lot to do with the amount of time she had spent away from the school helping us. We felt guilty for causing her to lose her job. Of course, at the school they were only paid sporadically, and Lana could make as much in two days being our hostess and interpreter as she could in a month teaching school. She bought a new carpet for the living room with the money she made as our interpreter and gave the old one, which was only two years old, to her sister. Sergei was also able to buy more stock in his company, becoming the largest stockholder in the closely-held company.

Since Lana was no longer at the Christian school, Anna could not go there for free. She enrolled in another school that specialized in English but did not have a special curriculum or satellite schools. That meant she did not have to go to school in the afternoon, and she began acting as our interpreter when we went to the orphanage. She became very good at finding us taxis and getting us around town. Sometimes we forgot that she was only nine years old.

We went to see the judge during his Tuesday office hours. He called us into his office first, even though there were several other people there to see him before we got there. He said three problems needed to be taken care of. First, he refused to work with our lawyer. We had to find another lawyer. Second, the application to adopt the girls was supposed to say that it was our duty to make sure the children remained Ukrainian citizens. The statement said child rather than children. Lana pointed out that the English version did say children but it had been translated incorrectly. He told us to make sure to tell Sue that the translation was wrong and they should look for a more competent translator next time.

Next he wanted copies of our bank statement. We had our income tax records, but not our bank statements. We had felt that it probably was not a good idea to give him anything with our bank account number on it. Although we told him that the income tax records were probably the most accurate representation of our income for the year, he still seemed to think it would be better if he had bank statements.

Finally, he said the documents for Irina were not right. The paper from the orphanage said that all three girls had been removed from their mother's custody, but the documents from the judge in Alexandria mentioned only Anastasia, Snijana, and their two older siblings. Irina had been born over two months after the others were removed from their mother's custody, then abandoned in the hospital. We would be required to produce corrected documents. Then he told us we could go.

Our lawyer Valerie found a new lawyer for us. Her name was Natasha. He would coach her in what to do. Natasha, Lana, and Valerie went to see the judge that afternoon. Lana was surprised and pleased when he agreed to set up a hearing date for later that week, if we corrected all the documents.

The judge had started a campaign of his own. There were many people in Kirovograd who thought like Lana's sister, that Americans could not be trusted. There had been numerous rumors of Americans buying children to provide organ donations for sick Americans. That was why my health was of such vital importance. A newspaper reporter approached Natasha and asked if she was defending an American couple who were accused of hurting adopted children. She told them she was helping us adopt children and sent the reporter to meet us. The reporter arrived with a negative attitude, but left four hours later with a positive attitude about the adoption, thanks to Lana.

The next day, Valerie started preparing a complaint against the judge to file with the regional judge. Apparently the district judge had made several legal mistakes, in addition to refusing to hold a scheduled hearing for no reason other than that he did not want to. We did not know all the reasons Valerie thought he had a legitimate complaint, but we did know that things were going on that would never be allowed in an American court.

We spoke with Sue almost every night and often what she had heard from Svetlana was different from what we had heard from Lana. Affairs were becoming ever more tangled and we were beginning to wonder whom to believe or how to act. We were, however, determined that we would persist as long as we had to and appeal as many times as was possible.

By this time we were feeling that spiritual warfare was being waged all around us. We sent e-mails to the people who were praying for us at home, and we prayed as we sat in the hallways. We prayed when we got up and when we went to bed. We prayed for the judge. We prayed that the girls would be ours by Christmas. We prayed that we would know the truth. Even though the situation was much more desperate than it had been the first week, when we had been discouraged about the error in the paperwork, we were not as disheartened as we had been then. We were much more angry, but never as disheartened.

We spent several hours every day sitting in the hallway at the courthouse trying to get in to see the judge. The hallway would have been condemned as a fire hazard in the United States. It was crammed with wooden chairs and benches and so many people that access to the stairs was almost impossible. There wasn't much to do but stare at the cracked and peeling paint, the lights that didn't work, and occasionally walk to the window at either end to stare at the bare trees and bleak sky. Lana and Svetlana spoke with the other people there, but most of them did not speak English. Sometimes we were able to see the judge, sometimes not. Some days he would see only Lana, and they would play word games with threats and counter threats. He hinted around his need for a bribe of seven thousand dollars. We refused to pay it.

Thursday, the day the hearing was scheduled, the Judge said he needed some more documents before he could proceed. We produced them by that afternoon, but he was in another hearing by that time. Our hearing was re-scheduled for Monday, a week after the original date.

On Monday, December 15, we met with the Regional Judge, who told us that the District Judge would give a favorable decision at our hearing at 11:30 a.m. the next day. At 11:30 the next morning he did in fact start the hearing. It was a very small courtroom. The bench was much like a court-room in the United States, stretching across the entire front of the court-room. There were three chairs behind the bench. The judge sat in the center one. Two tables for the defendant's lawyers were crammed in front of it, and off to the side was a cage to hold the prisoner in a criminal trial. On the other side, there were tables for the recording secretary and prosecuting attorney. The bar was pushed up against these tables, leaving about ten feet of space between the bar and the bench. At the entrance to this area was the "witness stand." This was a three-inch high plywood platform with a raised shelf in front of it sort of like a podium. Behind the witness stand were three rows of bench-style seating. There were also benches along the side of the room. East-facing windows lined one wall, so that the room was well lit and more pleasant than other areas in the courthouse. We had no trouble seeing people's faces, as we had in the hallway and the judge's office.

After calling the courtroom to order, the judge called roll of the people who were supposed to be there. The Orphanage Inspector was not there. The judge had neglected to subpoena both the Inspector and Luba. We had discovered this "oversight" and had informed both of them of the hearing. Luba showed up, but the Orphanage Inspector did not. The judge set another hearing for December 18. Then he invited us into his chambers and accused us of delaying the proceedings and wasting his time. In the two days before the next hearing Lana was to retranslate all the documents. The judge said he would hold her criminally responsible for their accuracy, and if there were any errors, she would go to jail.

That night Sue and Tom called from ICA. Some of our credit cards had been stolen. Robert and I had deliberately been carrying different credit cards, so if my purse or his wallet were stolen we would still have a credit card we could use. We had left the duplicate cards at home. Apparently a former foster daughter had broken into our house and taken the credit cards we had left there. She later came into the office wearing clothes she had charged to the credit cards. Our staff became suspicious, knowing she did not have the money to spend on those clothes. My mother checked our house and discovered that the cards were missing. She called ICA to have them contact us. My mother and ICA handled the cancellation of the credit cards, but we were left with only one valid card and it was within three hundred dollars of the credit limit. We were no longer prepared for an emergency.

Lana worked late into the night translating the documents and double-checked them the next day while we visited the girls. It was −30° Celsius outside and they did not have school, because it was too cold for walking. Lana called us a taxi, and nine-year-old Anna went with us as our translator. By this time, we had a regular taxi driver whom Lana would ask for whenever we needed to go somewhere. He was very helpful and interested in our situation. His wife was very ill, and he had two young children to care for, which was one reason Lana had selected him to be our personal driver. He really needed the money.

After a conversation with the lawyers that day, Lana told us that the judge was doing everything he could to make himself look good in the media and with the leaders of the community. She said he planned to ask us if we trusted him. If we said yes, it would be difficult to get an appeal. We had said we trusted him, so why should we question his decision. If we said no, he would most definitely deny the adoption. After a long discussion Lana told us to say, "We are believers in God. If a priest comes to us and asks if we believe in him, we must say we believe in God. The same is true here. We can only believe in Ukrainian law, not the person who sits in judgement."

On December 18 the judge issued the required summons to the Orphanage Inspector. She showed up this time. At that session, Valerie tried to give Natasha some advice, and the judge banished Valerie from the courtroom. Then the judge insisted that he needed a representative from the Center for International Adoptions present. That meant someone would have to come down from Kiev. He recessed the hearing until we could get someone there. Svetlana called Kiev. Lyudmilla, the Assistant Director of the

Center for Adoptions, had close friends in Kirovograd and agreed to be present at the next hearing.

By the time we had an official hearing with all the required people present it was December 19. We had rehearsed answers to some of the toughest questions Svetlana could remember from previous hearings, and she thought we were prepared. The judge started by asking if we wanted to reject the court. If we had said yes, we would have had to have started over at a different court, and he would have used his influence to see that it did not go well. We said we did not wish to reject the court. He asked us about an offer of a seven thousand dollar bribe he had supposedly received. We said we did not know anything about it. He asked us if we had any lawyer other than Natasha, and we told him about Valerie. Then he asked for the qualifications of everyone in the room. Each of the people there had to stand up and say their name, give their passport number, which was sort of like a citizenship number, where they worked, and state their qualifications.

Robert and I stood up and stated why we wanted the children, what our income was, and how we would take care of the children. Then he asked me if the rights of Ukrainian children would be protected in the United States and if, as adopted children, they would have the same rights as children born to us. I told him that they would. He pressed for whether they would have all the rights of children born in the United States. I told him they could never be President of the United States but that was the only right they would not have.

Next he started asking Lyudmilla questions. He insisted that the documents had been falsified because Irina's document said she had been removed from the mother's custody when she had actually been abandoned in the hospital when she was born, two months later. They argued over that; then Lyudmilla lectured him on the situation of orphans in Ukraine and specifically in Kirovograd where there had been no international adoptions in ten years and no adoptions at all in two years. Next he asked her where in the law it says how to prepare the statements. There is not a law concerning the preparation of the documents, it is only a Center for Adoption procedure, and in our case it had been followed as closely as possible. The judge started yelling at Lyudmilla about the law, which she had no part in creating.

The judge made her sit down and started asking the Orphanage Inspector some questions about the "falsified" documents. He also said the girls' father had not relinquished his rights in Irina's case, and the judge wanted to know why not. The Inspector told him that the father had not been present when they were relinquished and they weren't even sure Irina had the same father as the other children, since he had been in prison for several months before she was born. The judge recessed the court and until 1:30 p.m. and asked the orphanage inspector to have an explanation of the discrepancies in the documents by then.

We went to lunch at Lana's house while Svetlana and Misha drove the Orphanage Inspector to her office to look at the documents. On the way home, Lana said she was sure the judge was going to say no but something was stopping him. Could it be the prayers of hundreds of people around the world? When court started again at 1:30 p.m., the Orphanage Inspector had an explanation for what the judge considered discrepancies in the documents. He seemed very angry, and probably would not have accepted the explanation, if Lyudmilla had not stood up and said something to him. That diverted his attention to her. He asked her about the rights of adopted foreign children in America. Lyudmilla said that both the United States and Ukraine had signed a convention on the rights of children and that the children would have all the rights of citizens in the other country. He shouted at her for some time, and she managed to maintain her composure under his barrage. Then he said he needed a document from the United States government saying that this was so and recessed the hearing until 10:00 a.m. Monday morning.

Lyudmilla followed the judge to his office and asked if we could have a hearing the next day if we could get a fax from the United States Consulate by 3:30 p.m. He said we could, so we hurried to Lana's house where Lyudmilla called her office at the Center for Adoptions. They contacted the consulate immediately and had the document faxed to Sergei's office. Sergei came bounding up the steps at the courthouse with the official paper just before 3:30, quite pleased to be the hero of the day. Again the judge was dumbfounded that we had been able to meet his requirements. It was taking all the efforts of ICA and all the favors that our Ukrainian friends could pull in, but we were doing it.

When we presented the judge with the document, he said we needed a statement from the Center for International Adoptions saying that no one else had tried to adopt the girls. We had that faxed by 5:00 p.m., but he said he needed an original. Svetlana and Misha drove back to Kiev that night to get it while Lyudmilla stayed with friends in Kirovograd, and we resumed our routine of solitaire and visits to the orphanage.

After Valerie conferred with Natasha and Svetlana, prior to Svetlana leaving for Kiev, he came over to talk with us. He recommended that we reject that court and have the case heard by the Regional Judge. Lyudmilla and ICA were going to see what they could do over the weekend, and we would go visit the Regional Judge on Monday. The District Judge had said he would make a decision when he felt it was right in his heart, but Valerie said there was a little bag for money right next to his heart. Lana had learned that someone else, upset by the judge's misuse of power, had "accidentally" spilled acid all over his car, and the acid ate through the metal, ruining the car. The District Judge needed seven thousand dollars to get a new car

For the entire weekend, Svetlana, Lana, Sergei, Lyudmilla, Valerie, Natasha, Sue, and everyone else worked on strategies and ideas to make things go our way. They even made an appointment with a media consultant to discuss putting the case on T.V. The consultant would help determine how to present the case so the majority of Ukrainian people would be on our side. We continued to pray and asked Valerie to have his Evangelical church pray for us.

On Sunday night there was an ice storm.

Chapter 25

Do not be afraid for I am with you. I will bring your children from the east and gather you from the west. Isaiah 43:5

When we woke up Monday morning, Robert showed me the verses for that day, December 22, in his devotional book. It included Isaiah 43:5, "Do not be afraid for I am with you. I will bring your children from the east and gather you from the west." Although I had almost completely stopped reading the Bible study I had brought, Robert clung to his and continued to draw hope from it. By showing me that verse he turned my sight back to God and away from my frustration with the circumstances and obstacles we were facing. We had to walk to the courthouse that morning on streets coated with two inches of ice. The temperature was −10° Celsius and the wind was blowing almost hard enough to knock me over. We started early so we would be there on time.

We weren't sure if Svetlana could make it back from Kiev. At 10:00a.m. she and the Orphanage Inspector were still not there. The judge came to the courtroom, but since they were not there, he asked his assistant to let him know when everyone was present. We went outside and saw Svetlana just driving up. When we told her that the Orphanage Inspector had not arrived, so she and her driver went to get her. They all showed up very soon after that and the judge started the hearing. He briefly questioned Luba, asked the Orphanage Inspector some more questions, then interrogated Lyudmilla for some time. Lana was unable to translate the exchange quickly enough, but Lyudmilla was in tears when she sat down.

It seemed the Orphanage Inspector, the Center for International

183

Adoptions, and even the Mayor of Kirovograd were more on trial than we were. The judge accused them of falsification of documents and incompetence all around. After several minutes, I stopped paying attention to the proceedings, which Lana was unable to translate completely anyway, and just began praying. Soon Robert was also praying. Almost immediately there was a change in the demeanor of the judge. He asked us to make a statement about why we wanted to adopt the children, and we were allowed to summarize our case. Then he demanded more documentation from the orphanage inspector and recessed the court until 1:30 p.m.

We all walked back to Lana's apartment for lunch. It was safer to walk than to drive, but even walking had its hazards. Lyudmilla had fallen earlier on the ice, and she held tightly to Lana's elbow. Robert caught me and kept me from slipping a couple of times. He was really glad he had bought some new heavy-soled shoes and a down coat while we were in Albuquerque at Thanksgiving time. We barely had enough time to eat some soup and bread and walk back to the courthouse because our progress was so slow.

At 1:30 p.m. the judge accepted the document from the orphanage inspector, asked Natasha a couple of questions, then recessed us again until 3:30 p.m. We made another trek across the ice and waited nervously at Lana's house. Finally we went back to the courthouse. The judge asked us to stand, asked a couple of questions, then started reading from a paper. Lana didn't translate as he read. For the first few paragraphs Svetlana, Luba, Lana, Lyudmilla, and Irina were frowning. Then they looked angry, and finally they got very excited.

"The girls are yours," Lana whispered.

We were numb. At first we didn't realize it was over. When the judge had asked us to stand, we hadn't realized it was so he could read his decision. We were waiting for more questions.

In Ukraine there is a ten-day waiting period between the date a court decision is handed down and the day it goes into effect. We had been told about this and told to ask to have that waiting period waived. As we stood there Lana whispered, "Ask him to waive the waiting period." We nodded.

"You have to say it," Lana whispered.

"Please ask him," I said, still stunned by the decision.

Lana thanked the judge for his decision and made the request to get the girls immediately. The request was denied. Despite the fact that the girls were our daughters, we could not take them out of the orphanage for another ten days.

As the judge left the courtroom, everyone had to remain standing quietly, but as soon as he left they started congratulating and hugging us. It was only then that we realized he had actually granted the adoption. We knew it was God, through the prayers of many people, who had granted us the adoption. The judge had struggled against it the whole time but had been unable to overcome the prayers of the several hundred people who were praying for us in the United States and around the world.

The battle had taken its toll on everyone. Lyudmilla was emotionally exhausted and had somehow incurred the wrath of the director of the Center for International Adoptions. Svetlana and Lana were not getting along very well, partly because Lana didn't always want to do things Svetlana's way and partly, I think, because Svetlana was jealous of Lana's ability to get things done that Svetlana could not. Lana had warned us to be careful about what we said to Sue at ICA because it would get back to Svetlana. She said

Svetlana did not think too highly of us and still had the power to make things difficult and hold up paperwork in Kiev. Although I know Svetlana was frustrated by the situation, I think she was more interested in getting everything processed and getting us out of the country as soon as possible, than in holding up the paperwork any more. At ICA in Washington, they were still committed to helping us, but our case was costing much more than they had charged us, and it was hard on everyone there to keep providing the support we needed.

At Lana's house we held a quick celebration, and Svetlana and Lyudmilla left for Kiev to start preparing the paperwork so the girls could leave the country. Two other families had also arrived to adopt children in Kiev.

Chapter 26

God sets the lonely in families. Psalm 68:6

Anastasia was angry at Mama and Papa for not coming to see her yesterday. Lately they had not been coming all the time. They said they were busy trying to work things out with the judge. She had heard Natasha say that the judge was a really bad man. Everybody laughed when Anastasia called him Judge Lucifer. She wasn't sure why they laughed because Lucifer was one of those really scary characters from stories. One of the nurses had threatened her once that if she did not behave Lucifer would come and carry her away. Before long, Lana was calling him Judge Lucifer when she talked with the caregivers and Mama and Papa.

Anastasia wished Pavlik would get better. His surgery had been weeks ago, and he still did not want to play with her very much. When he came into the room, most of the time his forehead was hot and his face looked red. Anastasia knew that was not good. Usually when people were hot and red, they had to sleep in the room behind the doctor's office so everybody would not get what they had. For some reason Luba kept letting Pavlik come to be with her and the other children even though he was sick.

Since Mama and Papa were not there, Anastasia decided she and Pavlik should go down to the kitchen and see if they could get the cook to give them any chicken broth. Chicken broth was usually good for hot, red people. Just as they were about to leave, Mama and Papa came with Lana.

"Judge Lucifer said yes to the adoption," Lana said. "Your Mama and Papa will soon take you home to America soon. You also have new names now."

"What is my name?" asked Anastasia.

"Anastasia Marie Habiger-Doxon," said Lana.

She pronounced it in a really funny way.

"I don't like that name," Anastasia said. "If I am going to be an American, I need an American name."

Lana talked with Mama and Papa.

"Ana?" Mama said.

Anastasia did not like that. She shook her head.

"Marie?" Mama said.

Anastasia shook her head.

"Stacy?" asked Papa.

That was perfect. Anastasia nodded and clapped her hands.

"Okay, Stacy," Mama said. Anastasia understood her perfectly. She was very pleased with her American name and hoped they would leave for America soon.

Next, they told Snijana that her name was now Janalyn. She liked her name right away. Of course she did. Snijana liked everything. They told her she would be nicknamed Jana. She smiled again and hugged Mama.

They told Irina that her name was Lydia now. When they called her Lydia though, she didn't come. Anastasia didn't think Irina would ever get used to her new name. Irina liked things to stay the same.

After they had worked out the names, Lana went to talk with Natasha and Sveta. When Natasha heard that the judge had agreed to the adoption, she burst into tears.

"I didn't think they would get the girls," she cried. "I have had dealings with the judge and lost. I thought the adoption would be denied, and the girls would be traumatized."

Mama and Papa were really happy today. They didn't have time to play for long though. They had to go visit some other offices, so they left very soon.

Luba and Sveta were taking some of the kids to the older kids' orphanage. Pavlik was going and had asked if Anastasia could come along. Luba agreed. They all climbed into the orphanage van. The drive was not very far. By now Anastasia was an expert at going out into the city. She told the four year olds not to be afraid. When they got to the new orphanage, she announced to them "This is where you are going to live. I am going to live in America."

They went inside. Anastasia wanted to make sure the staff at this new orphanage knew that she would not be staying. "These are the kids who are coming here to live," she said, pointing to the small group of four-year-olds behind her. "I am going to America."

Chapter 27

In all your ways acknowledge God he will make your paths straight.
Psalm 3:6

To make the day special for us, Lana asked if the girls could spend Christmas with us. At least it was our Christmas. Despite the fact that just about every other day is some kind of holiday in Ukraine, December 25 is not. Their Christmas comes in January. Luba agreed that the girls could come to Lana's apartment for two hours. We scrambled to be ready. Anna took us to the most elite toy store in Kirovograd. After we examined and played with every toy in the shop, we picked a little turtle with different colored blinking lights on its back that played "Twinkle, Twinkle, Little Star" for Lydia. For Jana, we bought an animal matching game; for Stacy we found a doll with eyes that opened and closed. Anna returned again and again to the stuffed toys, where she looked longingly at a stuffed cat. While I distracted her in the back of the store, Robert bought it. We also bought wrapping paper and transparent tape. It was not traditional to wrap gifts in Ukraine. When we got home, Lana asked me to show her how to wrap gifts. Lana did not have scissors so we had to fold the paper and cut it with a knife, and they did not have boxes for the gifts, so they made rather lumpy packages. After I showed Lana how to wrap the girl's gifts, I secretly wrapped a Pueblo bear fetish from Albuquerque for Sergei, and a large cubic zirconia for Lana. Valerie and his family came over, too. We gave him a cowboy hat and bolo tie along with the Ukrainian recording of the Bible. He told us he would share the Bible recording with his church and thought he could get someone to put it on the radio.

All the gifts were wrapped, and everything was ready before noon. We had to wait until after naptime to pick up the girls. Sergei drove us to the orphanage. This time Lydia didn't scream quite so loudly in the car, and by the time we got to the apartment, she was just whimpering. Although she nearly choked me, I was able to hold her by myself. Jana announced that she needed to go to the bathroom as soon as we got in the car. Stacy recognized that Sergei's Mercedes was a better car than Misha's Toyota. She announced, "I am going to get a car like it as soon as I get to America."

At the red lights Stacy and Jana competed to see who could yell out *zipiniti* or *iti* fastest.

When we got to the apartment, we changed the girls into the Christmas outfits, green velvet for Stacy and Jana, and green and white ruffled Swiss dots for Lydia. The size-three dress was way too big for Lydia, and she pouted at having it on. We ate tangerines and candy, opened presents and had a whirlwind two-hour party. Then we had to put them back into their orphanage clothes, put their presents away, and take them back to the orphanage. All of us felt bereft when they were gone.

The girls were now our daughters. When the waiting period was over, we would get new birth certificates and passports for the girls. With those in hand we could go to Kiev, where we would get approval for them to leave the country, then to Warsaw, where we would get visas for them to enter the United States. Then, at last, we would be on our way home.

The situation was becoming critical at the office. The clients were agitated, the employees irritated, the income reduced to a dribble. Robert definitely needed to go home soon. Another two weeks in Ukraine could be critical to the success of the business. He had to go home if he was going to keep his employees and clients.

Lana advised us to be careful, since something had gone wrong at every other turn in the process. Svetlana, on the other hand, said everything was going to be fine now; she didn't anticipate any more delays. Sue told us to visit the offices that would issue the passports and birth certificates, to make sure we could get the paperwork we needed, before Robert left.

The day after Christmas we visited the office that issued new birth certificates. They assured us that there would be no problem getting birth certificates and that only the adoptive mother had to be present. Next we went to the passport office and were assured that if we brought in the adoption decree and the birth certificates it would take about an hour to get the passports and we would be on our way. No one in Kirovograd anticipated any problem if Robert left. Robert was very anxious to leave. I was much less confident, although once again everyone assured me that the things that remained were mere formalities and could be taken care of quickly and easily.

Valerie asked us to write a statement about all the things the judge had put us through, to be registered with the Regional Judge, once we had everything finished. As we were discussing the things to put in the statement, we discovered just how much effort Sergei, the reporters we had talked to, and the Assistant Mayor had made for us. We had thought we had been involved in every decision, but now we learned that a great deal had happened without our knowledge. Sergei had talked several times with the Regional Judge, who supervised the district court system, and even the Ministry of Justice representative in that region. The Regional Judge had needed his car fixed but did not have the money to pay for it. Sergei had gotten the car fixed and told the mechanics that the Regional Judge could have the car back and pay later. Lana had met several times with the first Assistant Mayor, and she had used all the influence she had to get the District Judge to make a decision.

We made an appointment to visit the Assistant Mayor to present her with a gift. This was the first time we had gone to the third floor of City Hall. Once before we had been allowed on the first floor, but most of our business had been conducted in the basement. We climbed the bare marble steps from the first floor. On the second floor the steps were carpeted with attractive oriental carpet runners. The third floor hallway had thick red carpeting and velvet curtains on the windows.

The Assistant Mayor's office was not the most luxurious one we had seen in Ukraine, but it was one of the neatest and most tastefully decorated. She had a lovely flower arrangement on her polished walnut conference table. We sat around the table and had tea, then we presented her with a silk scarf as a gift for her efforts. She gave us several brochures about Kirovograd and showed us one in which the Mayor was pictured with several children from the orphanage. There, in the glossy, professional looking brochure about Kirovograd, was Snijana sitting on the Mayor's lap. She asked us to have some important people in our own city send "thank you" letters to the Mayor for his part in helping us get the girls.

Chapter 28

If you believe, you will receive whatever you ask for in prayer. Matthew 21:22

I was very troubled that Robert had to leave, although I understood the urgency of the situation in Albuquerque. I was afraid I that when I got to Kiev there would be more foul-ups with the paperwork and I would be stuck there with the girls and with no one I could really talk to. Robert, on the other hand, was eager to go home and kept telling me that there was hardly anything left to do and that it surely couldn't go wrong. We made plans for him to return to Ukraine and travel with us in early January. He wrote out a statement saying I had full power to act on his behalf. Lana translated it, and we had it notarized.

Robert had four goals in mind when he left. First, he would express our thanks to everyone back home who had helped us in the adoption through finances, through prayer, and through taking care of our affairs at home. Second, he would determine the status of each of his projects at work and determine how to proceed with the business, after having been gone most of the last three months. Third, he would prepare for a talk he was to give at a regional conference in Phoenix that would pave the way for future work, and fourth, he would try to find some money. We had outlined our financial needs to get the girls home, and it amounted to $1500 more than we had.

He left at 4:00 a.m. on December 29, Lydia's birthday. Since she was barely tolerating him at this point, she would not miss him. He arrived at the Borispol airport at 7:30 a.m., where he planned to buy a one-way ticket to Warsaw, then find some breakfast. Once in Warsaw he would arrange for a round trip ticket to Albuquerque and back using his frequent flyer miles. By now he was familiar with the airport, which was important because the people who had driven him from Kirovograd could not speak English. He went to the airport office to purchase his ticket. The woman there spoke only broken English, but she could understand what he needed.

"Yes. Ticket to Warsaw available," she said. "Two hundred eighty dollars American."

Robert was relieved because he had thought he might have to delay the trip until a seat was available or that it might cost more than the credit left on his MasterCard.

Robert gave the woman behind the desk his credit card and asked her to book the flight. She ran the card through the machine and start-ed talking rapidly to the driver. All Robert could make out was "Master Card" and "*Nyet.*" Finally she said, "Card stolen. Not give back."

"There was a mistake," Robert explained. "Some of my credit cards were stolen, but not this one. I had this one here."

"Card not work," she said. "Stolen. Not give back."

Just as he was beginning to think he might be spending some time in a Ukrainian jail rather than returning to the United States, a woman approach-ed and asked, "Can I be of assistance?"

Robert explained the situation to her, trying not to appear too anxious or frustrated. He knew she was trying to decide if he was telling the truth, or if he was a dangerous criminal with a stolen credit card. She decided he could be trusted and took him to the airline's main office. It was in an area of the airport most people never see.

Robert again explained that somehow the MasterCard had been reported stolen rather than the Visa, which should have been canceled. Even if they believed him, he could not charge on that card because MasterCard would not allow it. He pulled out the Visa card.

"See if this one will work. Maybe they canceled the wrong card."

If this one did not work, he would have to come up with plan C, and he had no idea what that would be.

The Visa card worked, and he got his ticket. Everyone in the office hugged him and kissed him on both cheeks in Ukrainian fashion, and he was escorted back to the lobby. By now it was too late to get any breakfast or do anything other than check his luggage, show his papers at the four check-points he had to pass through, and get on the plane.

On the way to Warsaw he studied his Warsaw travel guide, checked out hotel descriptions, and found the locations of the US Embassy and the American Airlines ticket office. The Marriott seemed a safe choice, because it was within walking distance, at least by European standards, of all the places he needed to visit the next day. By the time he arrived he felt reassured that everything would work out. The city was even more beautiful than he had imagined, and the taxi to the hotel took him by several interesting neighborhoods and parks. That night he called me and told me that the Master-Card had been canceled. I grew even more demoralized. After a good night's sleep in a soft bed in a western-style hotel, he was full of confidence and ready to tackle whatever came his way.

First he walked to the American Airlines ticket office. Robert told the clerk that he wanted to use his frequent flyer miles to travel the next day to Albuquerque and return to Warsaw ten days later. He wanted to go through London and Chicago with no long layovers in either city. The clerk started to laugh.

"Tomorrow is New Year's Eve," he said. "There is no way you will be able to travel tomorrow."

Robert asked him to check anyway and said a quick, silent prayer.

The clerk looked up from the computer. "I can't believe it," he said. "You can do exactly what you wanted. I checked yesterday, and there was no space on this flight."

Robert knew that God had answered his prayer.

He arrived home on January 1, 1998, after an uneventful twenty-hour flight and went right to bed. He was awakened the next morning by a phone call telling him that his first grandson had been born.

The judge's decree would be final ten days after December 22, which happens to be January 1. New Year's is the biggest holiday in Ukraine, and of course everything would be closed for four days for the holiday.

Lana and I prepared a request for six copies of the adoption decree, complete with original signatures and the proper seals, and took it to the judge. With advance notice the proper number of copies might be prepared, and we might not have to wait while they retyped the decree. When Lana gave him the requests, he shouted at her first for several minutes. Lana threatened to jump out of the window of his second-floor office. He threatened to put her in jail. Then he demanded a statement saying we didn't have anything against him and wanted to know why we had made complaints against him. He had either heard about Valerie's intended complaint or expected that something like that might happen.

After about half an hour of threats and counter threats they made peace, and he invited me into his office. He led Lana and me to the back of the office and pushed on one of the panels in the wall. It opened to reveal a narrow room with a cot, a little table, an office-size refrigerator and a bar sink. We sat at the table, and he poured champagne for Lana and me.

"To you and your daughters," he said. "I just want what is best for the girls."

We drank. Lana proposed a toast to his health.

"Happy New Year and good luck with the children," he said.

We were obviously not the first ones with whom he had shared a few drinks in honor of the coming New Year. Lana asked him what the decree said, and he replied that he had not written it yet. That worried me. Would we be able to get our six copies of the decree when the court reopened after New Years?

Lana and I wrote a paper that evening that said we really had nothing against the judge. I tried to word it as carefully as I could, so that I did not say I approved of the tactics of the judge or really thought he was a good guy.

While Lana was translating my statement, Tom called from ICA. Svetlana had said the statement Robert wrote giving me power of attorney was not worded right. They would need a power or attorney executed in the United States and worded according to specific requirements to process the remaining paperwork. It would cost five hundred dollars to process the power of attorney.

"I think Svetlana really needs an extra five hundred dollars and is using this request for a power of attorney to get it," I told Tom. "Our funds have been exhausted, our remaining credit cards extended to their limit, we have no idea where we will get the extra fifteen hundred dollars we need in

Warsaw and our emotions are drained. I simply cannot come up with another five hundred dollars."

"I have talked with Robert," he told me. "He expects to have the power of attorney completed tomorrow and will send it to me with the five hundred dollars."

I was furious that the requirements kept changing, or were not communicated to us accurately, and every time we turned around we needed more money.

On the morning of New Year's Eve, Lana and I went to the market on the way to see the girls. Because it was New Year's Eve, the money-changing booth was closed. A small group of young men was loitering near the booth. One of them approached Lana.

"I will exchange money for you," he said. "I offer a very favorable rate," he held out his hand. Lana handed him the bill, and he folded it up. Two of the other young men started a sort of shoving match, and one hit the man with the one hundred dollar bill in the shoulder. Lana realized what was happening and tried to grab the one hundred dollar bill back. He quickly slipped a folded one dollar bill into her hand and ran away. She ran after the man, yelling at him. I followed. Some taxi drivers stopped him, and Lana managed to catch up. I was a little slower, but when I caught up with them Lana was berating him. She threatened to have him put in jail for stealing a one hundred dollar bill from an American, and there were plenty of witnesses to testify that he did it. Lana told everyone, in a loud voice, that we were the ones who had already gotten the head district judge to decide in our favor. Other taxi drivers were getting out of their cars to see what was going on. The would-be thief gave the money back and ran away.

The whole experience shook me. I was down to four hundred dollars by this point and was feeling very vulnerable. I wouldn't be able to get a cash advance on my credit cards even when I did get to Kiev, where hotels could give cash advances. Since the MasterCard had been canceled, I was left without a source of emergency cash.

Lana was exhilarated by the close call. For two hours we toured the market, and Lana told the story of our adventure to all her friends. It grew each time she told it. We finally went to the orphanage and spent a little time with the girls, then went home to prepare New Year's dinner for Lana's family and their guests.

New Year's Eve started pleasantly enough for me. Sergei's new driver came over for dinner. They had met at the seashore during the summer and had agreed at that time to celebrate New Years together. In the fall, when Sergei's driver became unreliable, he fired him and was looking for a new driver. He remembered his friend from the seashore and hired him. We had a great time and celebrated until about 2:00 a.m. Then, other friends of Sergei's called and invited us over, so we walked to their house. They were much louder and somewhat vulgar. I couldn't understand the words they were saying, but the implications of their looks and gestures were quite clear. I have never been comfortable in situations like that, and I desperately wanted Robert to be with me. About 4:30 a.m. we walked back to Lana and Sergei's and had tea and cake. We had left Anna and the driver's two children at their house watching television, and they had fallen asleep on the floor. Sergei soon fell asleep with the children. I went to my room to sleep, but Lana and the others went for a walk downtown to watch the sun come up on the New Year, then played cards until the children woke up. Lana finally went to bed about 10:00 a.m.

Chapter 29

Blessed are the pure in heart, for they will see God. Matthew 5:8

"We are going to play airport," Anna explained. "Pretend you are in an airport getting ready to go to America."

That sounded like a fun game to Stacy. Mama gave her and Janalyn each a backpack and showed them how to put it on. She was beginning to understand the funny words Mama spoke. When Mama said, "Everyone hold hands while we walk. We all have to stay together," she understood. Lydia seemed to understand, too, but Anna had to tell Janalyn. They walked to the other end of the hall and sat on a bench outside the room there. Mama took some things out of the backpacks to play with, and they sat on the benches coloring and playing with the toys. Then they practiced going down the stairs. This was great fun. They went all over the orphanage.

Since they had been walking all around the orphanage, Stacy decided to take everyone to the kitchen to help get lunch for her room. She asked Sveta, who said that would be fine. Stacy led the way down the stairs and to the kitchen in the back of the orphanage. They waited outside the kitchen door while the cooks handed pots of food to the caretakers from each room. As the cooks were handing out food, the head cook came out of her office.

When she saw Mama, Anna, Janalyn and Lydia there, she started yelling, "Why are all these people here. Send them away. They will spread germs all over the entire orphanage."

Stacy couldn't understand that, because she came here all the time. When she and Pavlik came, they always let them into the kitchen and gave them little bits of extra food. She just wanted to introduce her Mama to her favorite cooks.

Natasha and Sveta decided to have a birthday party for Lydia because she had just turned three. They didn't usually have birthday parties, but they wanted to show Mama what a Ukrainian birthday party was like. First Mama and Lana drank champagne with all the caregivers. Lana let Stacy taste it, and she discovered she really liked champagne. Then, everyone played birthday games and sang a traditional birthday song while Lydia stood in the middle of the circle of singers. After Lydia had been in the center of the circle, Julia started yelling that she wanted a turn, so everyone else got a turn to be in the center even if it wasn't their birthday. Stacy didn't think that was fair, because it was Lydia's birthday. The Assistant Director gave Lydia a pink and white polka-dotted ball for a birthday present, and Luba gave her a copy of a book in Ukrainian. Stacy looked at the book and discovered it was her favorite story about the three goats. Then came the best part. Stacy and Janalyn ate chocolate with the grownups. Lydia couldn't have any because she would get sick if she ate it. Every time Lydia ate chocolate she got red bumps on her skin. Lydia and all the other kids ate the tangerines Mama and Lana had brought for them.

Stacy wondered whether she was truly going to America. They had said the adoption was final; they had taken her to Lana's apartment and celebrated. Now she was still waiting to leave with her Mama and Papa. And Papa wasn't even coming to the orphanage anymore. Mama was always holding Lydia and not paying any attention to Stacy. She really didn't like Mama that much but could accept her because she would get a Papa. But what if Papa was gone and all she ever saw now was Mama? On top of all that, Pavlik was sick. She felt his head and he had a fever, so she took him right to Luba's office.

"Please go back to your room, Stacy," Luba told her, frowning and holding Pavlik in a very troubled way. Stacy left the office but stayed right outside the door, peeking in. Pavlik was her brother and her future husband. If he was sick enough for Luba to worry, Stacy did not want to leave him.

Maybe Mama and Papa were waiting to take her home after the New Year's program. Stacy had a very big part in that. She knew that some of the other older children would be leaving for the other orphanage right after the program. They must need her for the program and would let her go after it was finished.

On the day of the program everyone was very excited. A lot of the orphanage patrons had come to see them. Father Christmas was there with his daughter, although Stacy knew they were both staff members dressed up, just like Yuri was dressed up as Father Time, and all the children were dressed up in costumes. There were Christmas trees all over the orphanage. Lydia got to be a snowflake in this program and dance with the Ice Queen. In one act Stacy, Janalyn, Pavlik and Yuri would be penguins. In another Janalyn was a fox chased by several boys who were rabbits.

Pavlik did a great job with the welcoming speech, even though she knew he was still sick. He was looking worse all the time. As they were getting into their penguin costumes, Pavlik collapsed. Natasha ran off to get Luba. When Luba came, she and the doctor carried Pavlik away. Stacy started to follow them but they made her go on. They did the penguin show without Pavlik. Janalyn said Pavlik's lines, because she had memorized the whole program. Luba was already gone with Pavlik to the hospital, so the Assistant Director said good-by to everyone. She apologized and said there was an emergency, so everyone left in a rather sad mood. When the program was over, they all went to sit on Mama's lap. Stacy left as soon as she could to find out about Pavlik.

On New Year's Day Mama didn't come. Janalyn said she probably went home, too, but Lydia said "*Nyet*" to that. It was a very quiet day at the orphanage. Luba and Pavlik did not come. Stacy awoke to someone crying in the outer room. She slipped out of bed and walked out to see Natasha, Sveta and Irina talking quietly.

"What is the matter?" she asked.

"Pavlik died last night," they told her.

"Why did he die?" Stacy was stunned.

"He had a kidney infection. Luba didn't have enough money to get the right medicine," they told her.

Stacy walked quietly back to her bed, hid her head under the covers and cried for her best friend.

Chapter 30

Commit your way to the Lord; trust in him and he will do this: He will make your righteousness shine like the dawn, the justice of your cause like the noonday sun. Psalm 37:5-6

Several of the orphanage staff blamed the judge for Pavlik's death. If our adoption had been completed two months sooner, ICA could have found him parents and a home in time for him to get the antibiotics he needed to fight the kidney infection, they reasoned. Everyone was very upset and subdued, even the staff at ICA in Washington, when we called and told them what had happened.

Strangely enough, the court was open on Sunday, January 4 after being closed for three days for the New Year holiday. Lana and I went to the courthouse at 8:00 a.m. that morning. The clerk asked us to wait for about ten minutes, while she got the key and unlocked the cabinet with the official documents that were ready for distribution. While we were waiting, we spoke with the typist in the hall. She had not received the statement from the judge yet. He came in shortly after that and gave her the document to type. When she started typing it, she had some questions about the names. Lana explained the names then read the document and found several errors. We took it upstairs to the judge and he said we could correct the errors. Then we waited until 10:00 a.m for the secretary to type it on an old, manual typewriter, with six carbons.

Svetlana and Natasha had briefed Lana about the statement. The last paragraph should state the court where the decision was made and where the original document can be found. That paragraph was missing and there were other things she questioned. Lana decided we needed to talk to Natasha about the statement. Our usual driver was not available, so we flagged down a taxi near the courthouse. This taxi had an unpleasant odor and was not very well taken care of, but we needed a ride as quickly as possible. Natasha's partner said she was at a hearing in another court, so we had the taxi driver take us to that court. Lana paid the taxi driver in advance to get him to wait for us. We sat on benches in the hallway of the other court and waited for Natasha. There was a totally different atmosphere in this courthouse. Although there was a certain amount of tension in the air and the building was shabbier, there wasn't the feeling of corruption and despair that we sensed in the other courthouse.

When Natasha's case recessed, we took her back to the district court. Our usual driver had heard that we needed him and was waiting for us outside the district courthouse, so we dismissed the old, smelly taxi and asked "our" driver to wait for us. Natasha talked to the judge, and he agreed to make the changes she suggested. Our driver took her back to the other courthouse in time to resume the hearing that was going on there, while Lana and the judge's assistant proofread the statement and found several more errors. The assistant let us into the office to talk him into getting those corrected. By now his assistant was on our side. We had just started explaining the errors when several men in black suits walked in unannoun-ced. He immediately told us to make whatever changes we thought necessary and waved us out of the office. Lana marked the changes, then the entire document had to be retyped.

By the time the six copies were ready for signatures the judge had left for lunch, so we walked to Lana's to have something to eat. When we got there, the water was off, and they hadn't notified Lana first like they usually do in that apartment building. She always kept a bucket of water handy for flushing toilets, which was helpful today, but fixing lunch took a little longer than expected because we could not use the instant bouillon cubes she had bought to make soup. We had sausage and a cabbage salad instead, so we were late returning to the courthouse.

We were nervous about being late to pick up the documents. The judge didn't need much of an excuse to refuse to let us have them. When we got there, we still had to wait for about half an hour for the papers to be signed. When the assistant gave them to us, Lana discovered that he had signed only the first one. She barged right back into his office, demanding signatures on all the copies. The documents then had to be registered and notarized. It was late afternoon by the time we left with six copies of the final decree. Now, I thought, the worst was over, and we would be leaving in three, maybe four days.

Natasha and Lana both said it was a very poor document, Natasha from a legal standpoint and Lana from a grammatical standpoint. It described the whole adoption process, including a statement that my doctor first said I would not be a good mother, then changed the statement but the judge had his doubts about whether that was right. My failure to get the health certificate corrected in the summer continued to haunt me. There was also a statement about discrepancies in the documentation about the girls. We hoped that would not cause problems later on.

With the papers in hand, we went to the orphanage to get the girl's original birth certificates. These would be destroyed when they made new birth certificates stating that I was the girl's mother and Robert was their father. Luba was making arrange-ments for Pavlik's funeral, and only she could give us the birth certificates. We decided to go to the office of the person who issued birth certificates anyway, just to make sure everything was in order. She was not there either, but Lana got her home phone number so we could set up a time to meet with her.

Our next stop was a bakery to order cake for the farewell party at the orphanage. The bakery was not a little shop on the corner somewhere, like all the places that sold bread. It was a huge commercial bakery in an indust-rial area on the edge of town. In all the tours of Kirovograd I had never been to this area before. Our driver parked in the yard outside, and we walked through the huge, deserted warehouse. We found the staff of five, all that was left in what had once been a major enterprise, sitting in the manager's office celebrating the recent baptism of her granddaughter. We asked for three cakes decorated with roses.

Lana asked me, "How many kilos?"

I had absolutely no frame of reference for ordering kilos of cake. I just knew how many dollars I had left.

"I'm not sure how many kilos. Just ask them to make about thirty dollars worth of cake," I replied. I found out when we picked them up later that thirty dollars worth of cake is a lot of kilos.

Next, we went back to the orphanage. Luba was there, congratulated us on getting the adoption decree, and gave us the birth certificates. As she was looking through her files, she asked, "What else do you think you might need?"

"Do you have any health records?" I asked. "And if you have any other information on the girls, I would really appreciate having it."

Luba gave me a copy of the decree removing Stacy, Janalyn, and their older brother and sister from their mother's custody, which includes their mother's full name and birthplace, and the girl's complete health records. This is much more than some parents get when completing a foreign adoption, so I was very pleased. Our final stop of the day was at a notary to get the papers from the orphanage notarized, but the notary wasn't there.

When we got home, Lana called Svetlana in Kiev and Irina in Washington and told them about the judge's statement. They said he probably made the qualifying statements in case there were problems later but that we would not have any problem if we got strong statements from the orphanage and Center for Adoptions supporting the adoption. Svetlana asked Lana to put one copy of the documents on the train, but she talked on the phone too long. She arrived at the train station fifteen minutes after the train left.

Monday, January 5, we went to talk to the person who issued birth certificates, hoping to get that done before the Orthodox Christmas holiday on January 7. Lana went into the office while I waited outside. When she came out, she said they would not issue the birth certificates, because the girls had a hyphenated last name. They had to have either the name of the father or the name of the mother. They could not have a combination of both.

Suddenly I was on the verge of tears. We could never count on anyone to be in their office; when they were in, we had to wait while they typed pages of documents on old, manual typewriters with carbon paper; and now they wouldn't even do what they had promised to do! Lana took me home then went back to the office. She and a woman who worked in the office spent the rest of the day trying to get something done but couldn't get the official in charge to agree to anything. We finally had to go back to the judge to ask him to change the girls' names.

That night I called Robert.

"You'll never believe what happened," he said. "On the morning of January 2, I walked into the office of St. Stephen's to fill the staff in on the latest developments. They said they had something for me," he said. "Jeff Lust, our new senior pastor, handed me an envelope. Jeff said some additional donations had come in for us, and that this was the full amount they had left in the account they had started for us. It was a check made out for $1600. With tears in my eyes, I told the staff that we had calculated that we needed $1500 to complete everything in Warsaw."

This was welcome news, but I knew the joy would evaporate as I explained that we couldn't get the birth certificates. After expressing his disbelief and frustration in a rather forceful manner, Robert said he would fax a statement saying that he did not mind if the girls had my last name. We thought that would be easier, because I was the one who was there. The fax man at Sergei's office delivered the fax that evening.

In the morning, we took the statement to the judge. The judge said if we wanted to change the girls' names we would have to submit a request to the Council of Judges. The Regional Judge, who was in charge of the Council, said it would take about four months to complete the name change. I couldn't believe this was happening, after they had told us that everything was in order and it would be a simple process to get the new birth certificates.

On January 6, Christmas Eve in Ukraine, we picked up our thirty dollarsd worth of cake. They were still decorating the cakes. I couldn't believe the speed with which the decorator made perfect roses, leaves and latticework on top of the cakes. It took six of us to carry the three enormous cakes to the car. Our next stop was the wholesale market near the bakery, where we bought a case of oranges, a case of bananas, some chocolate, and a case of champagne. We took them to the orphanage. The orphanage cooks had prepared sandwiches and wine to celebrate.

Chapter 31

There in the presence of the Lord you and your families shall eat and rejoice in everything you have put your hand to, because the Lord your God has blessed you. Deuteronomy 12:7

For once Janalyn didn't care that Stacy was making faces at her. Lana had just said, "Today you are leaving the orphanage. You will go to my house first, then your Mama will take you home to America." Stacy was making faces because she had been right all the time; they were going to go to America.

First Mama and Lana took Janalyn and her sisters into the sleeping room, where they took all of their clothes off, even their underwear, and put on their Christmas clothes. When they came back to the day room, all the other children were taken into the sleeping room. Janalyn felt really special. Luba poured champagne and everyone made toasts. Stacy asked if she and Janalyn could have some champagne. Mama shook her head, but Lana let them each have a little cup. Janalyn didn't like it much, but Stacy said she did.

Almost all the staff was there. Even a couple of the cooks came up. Before they knew it, the champagne was all gone. Then everyone ate the sandwiches and drank tea. Mama and Lana and Luba kept taking pictures of everything. They took pictures of all three girls behind the huge cakes. They cut one cake, and the adults ate some. Janalyn didn't want any because the last time she ate cake she had gotten sick. She didn't want to be sick on her first day with her Mama.

The caregivers were telling stories about them. Janalyn snuggled into the space between Natasha and Luba so she could listen better. She begged for them to tell about things she remembered. Some of the caretakers said Lydia didn't talk because of a problem with her tongue. Sveta's daughter Lara, who stayed with them at night, said Lydia could talk, she was just very shy.

They told stories about how Stacy made everyone laugh, and how talented Janalyn was in music and acting. Sveta made Mama promise to give her music lessons in America. They also said Stacy and Janalyn were always causing problems and that Mama needed to be very firm and strict with them. Janalyn didn't think she was so bad, but Stacy was. They shouldn't talk about her, when it was always Stacy who did the really bad things. Janalyn just didn't like to sit still.

Mama asked how Stacy was taking Pavlik's death. That made everyone sad. Luba told Mama that Stacy knew what had happened but was too young to really understand. No one had really talked to her about her feelings. Janalyn knew Stacy could understand, because Janalyn understood that Pavlik was dead but he would have been alive if the doctors had given him better medicine. The nurses talked about that all the time.

The grownups started to talk about the judge. They said Pavlik could have been adopted, and would have lived somewhere with proper medical care if the judge had not been so stubborn. Janalyn did not like it that they were talking about Pavlik and the judge at her party, so she climbed on Natasha's lap and whispered *"Ya tebya lyublyu,"* in her ear. Natasha took all three girls on her lap and told them how much she loved them, too.

Sveta, who had been trying to teach them a little English, had them say some words in English. Then they taught Mama "I have to go to the bathroom," "I am thirsty," and "I am hungry" in Ukrainian. Why didn't

Mama know even the simplest things?

At last it was time to go. Mama took Janalyn's hand and said, "Okay. *Paka* "

Janalyn and Mama proudly led a little parade out of the orphanage. Behind them came Stacy, holding hands with the two head nurses, followed by Natasha carrying Lydia. The rest of the staff, except for a few who had to care for the other children, followed with Luba and Lana bringing up the rear.

At the car everyone hugged and kissed the girls. Mama lifted Janalyn into the car, sat beside her and took Lydia from Natasha. Janalyn plugged her ears as Lydia began to scream. Stacy said *paka* to everyone again; then Lana got in and pulled Stacy onto her lap. Stacy and Janalyn stuck their heads out the car window waving and calling *paka* to everyone. Lydia screamed and most of the staff stood in the driveway crying. Jana thought this was a happy time. Why were so many people were crying because she got to go to America?

As they walked into Lana's apartment a yellow ball of fur rocketed at Janalyn. She screamed in terror and climbed up Mama's leg and into her arms with Lydia.

"It's just the poodle," said Lana. "He is being friendly. He won't hurt you."

But Janalyn was not about to get down until that animal was gone. Lydia was afraid of it, too. Lana put the dog on the porch for the night. The next day, before Janalyn got up, Anna took the dog to her grandparents.

They had a really nice dinner, but Mama made them stop eating before Janalyn was ready to quit. Mama said she didn't want her to get sick again.

After dinner, Mama took all three of them to the bathroom and filled the tub. Janalyn had never seen so much water in one place at one time. In the orphanage, once a week they stood in a dishpan and the caretakers poured water over their heads. That was the only bath they got. Stacy climbed right into the big tub. Janalyn watched Stacy, just to be sure. Stacy seemed to be having fun, so she climbed in. Then Mama tried to put Lydia in. Lydia screamed like Mama was trying to drown her. Janalyn was getting really tired of all that screaming. At the orphanage they would have hit her a long time ago. Sergei came to check what was happening and that scared Lydia so badly that she stopped screaming. Mama was able to hand her to Stacy, who splashed her gently with water and got her to enjoy the bath.

Then Mama started washing their hair. She washed Stacy's first. For some reason, Stacy was smiling while Mama rinsed the soap right into her face. Then Mama tried to put the yellow shampoo on Janalyn. She wasn't going to let Mama put stinging bubbles in her eyes. She started screaming and pushed Mama's hands away. But Mama was really strong and finally got the shampoo into Jana's hair. She started rinsing when Jana wasn't looking. Jana was so surprised. The bubbles didn't hurt her eyes. By this time, Lydia was thoroughly enjoying herself and let Mama wash her hair without even crying a little bit.

Mama used a sprayer on a hose to rinse their hair. As soon as she put it back on the holder, Stacy grabbed it, turned it on and began spraying Janalyn with it. Then Janalyn sprayed Stacy, but that also sprayed Mama. Mama tried to grab the sprayer, but Janalyn handed it back to Stacy, and they kept it away from Mama. Then they sprayed Lydia with it, and she laughed really hard. Stacy let Lydia hold the sprayer, and she sprayed Mama and the wall behind her, then the towels on the towel rack and the mirror above the sink. Mama turned off the water and got the sprayer away from Lydia.

Mama pulled Janalyn out of the tub first, wrapped her in a blanket and carried her to Lana to put on her pajamas. Stacy climbed out, and Mama carried Lydia and led Stacy into their room. When everybody was in their pajamas and ready for bed, Mama put them down in front of the TV and went to clean up the bathroom, but Anna had already cleaned it and was taking a bath.

Janalyn was falling asleep on Sergei's lap, so Mama carried her to bed then put the other two in the room with her. But Mama went back to watch TV. Janalyn and Stacy lay whispering. They didn't want to be in the room all by themselves. Who would take care of them?

Janalyn got up and told Mama she needed to go to the bathroom. After Mama took her to the bathroom and took her back to the bedroom, Stacy said she needed something to eat. Mama gave them all apples and put them back to bed. Soon Jana was up again because she was afraid to be left alone in a room without an adult. When Janalyn got up, Lydia got up, too and they went to find Mama. Mama finally came to bed with them, and they were able to go to sleep.

Anna's bed had been moved into the living room for Stacy to sleep in. They had pushed two chairs together for Janalyn to sleep in and Lydia would sleep with Mama. But Stacy and Janalyn didn't think it was fair for Lydia to get to sleep with Mama all the time. Besides, they knew Lydia kicked and moved all night. They knew it was hard to sleep with Lydia, so in the middle of the night Stacy had Lydia trade with her. Janalyn was really nervous that she would wet the bed, so she had to keep getting up to go to the bathroom. She was afraid of the dark and had to wake Mama up every time so she could have Mama turn on the light.

They slept very late the next morning. When they finally got up, Anna told them "It's Christmas. We are going to *Baba's* for Christmas dinner."

Everyone walked to Anna's *Baba* and *Tata's* house. Janalyn had never walked that far, and it seemed there were cats or dogs coming after them every time they turned a corner. Lydia was walking really slowly, but Mama wouldn't carry her. Finally Stacy convinced Sergei to walk ahead with Stacy, Janalyn and Anna and leave Mama and Lana to walk with Lydia. Janalyn still thought the walk would take forever, but they finally got to *Baba* and *Tata's* house.

Janalyn couldn't believe all the food on the table.

"It is a tradition for Christmas," explained Anna, while they waited for Mama, Lydia and Lana. "There are twelve dishes, one for each of the twelve apostles. None of them have meat in them. My favorite is the cherry gelatin."

Mama and Lana finally got there with Lydia. Janalyn was really glad they could finally start eating.

Baba tied big towels around their necks and dished food onto their plates. This was the kind of meal Janalyn liked. She could eat and eat. She hoped the meal would go on forever, but they finally said that was all of the food.

After dinner Sergei went to get the car and drove them home. That was certainly better than walking.

As soon as they walked into the apartment, Lana said, "Time to take a nap."

"We are too old for naps," Janalyn and Stacy insisted; but after Lana made them lie down and pulled the shades, they found that all that eating and all that walking really had made them tired, and they fell asleep right away.

Janalyn woke up when Mama came into the room looking for something. She held the iron but couldn't find the ironing board. Mama finally started ironing on the floor. The iron tipped over on Lana's new rug. Mama grabbed it right away but the hot iron had already melted an iron shaped spot on the rug. It was right in front of the door, too, where it would be obvious. Janalyn could see that Mama was upset. She told Lana she would buy a new rug but Lana just said they would turn it around. That would put the spot under the big potted palm where nobody would see it.

That night Lana put the little potty in their room so Janalyn would not have to turn on the lights and wake everyone. That was really nice because she wouldn't even have to leave the room to go to the bathroom. She still had to wake Mama up though, because she wanted help pulling down her pants and making sure she did not spill the little pot.

Chapter 32

Ask and it will be given to you, seek and you will find, knock and the door will be opened. Matthew 7:7

All the holidays were over, at least for the next eight weeks, so all offices would be open. Lana's mother babysat the girls while Lana and I returned to our quest for birth certificates. The Soviet system had inspired some very creative ways of thinking. Although the regional official still wasn't willing to issue a birth certificate with a hyphenated last name, she had read the paperwork carefully and discovered that the documents listed the birthplace as the Alexandria district. She called the officials in Alexandria and informed them they would have to issue birth certificates for us. They said they would be happy to. The official in Kirovograd was very glad to have gotten out of a potentially difficult situation, and the person in Alexandria, who had read about the adoption in the paper, was pleased to have a part in the drama.

Now the only obstacle was getting to Alexandria. Our driver was concerned about his children, at home with his sick wife. Lana gave him some money for gas and told him to go home and check on his wife. He took us to Lana's house to get food while he filled the gas tank and checked on his family.

Alexandria is about one hundred kilometers away from Kirovograd. It was a pleasant drive through bare wheat fields and tree-lined pastures. We drove up the broad, empty streets lined with buildings that were all less than three stories high. There was much less institutional Soviet influence in Alexandria than in Kiev or Kirovograd. Something about the city reminded me of a town in a Western movie. Our car was the only one in sight.

The officials were waiting for us in the office. In this small town, the office normally would not have been open the day after Christmas, but having an American come to visit was quite an occasion. Everyone who worked there and several of their friends, stopped by to see us while we were there. As soon as we arrived, the senior official called her daughter, a high school student, who rushed right down. She walked in; her mother took one look at her and started scolding her about the lipstick she was wearing. Ukrainian teenagers are not that different from American teenagers, and neither are their mothers. Her school did not specialize in English, but she could speak it fluently. She said she learned more English from watching American movies than from her English classes in school.

After several minutes of visiting in the outer office, the senior official signaled her assistant and invited Lana and me into the inner office. The assistant followed and locked the door. In this office there was a wooden desk, a wall unit on one side, bare wood floors, and a safe in the corner. After the door was securely locked, the safe was unlocked. The safe was filled with identical blue books with removable covers like photo albums. The official found the book recording births between 1990 and 1997. As the assistant was taking the book out, the senior official asked for Robert's and my marriage certificate. I only had one certified copy left. Lana talked with her for some time, and she agreed to accept a copy. They would make the copy after the births were recorded.

The senior official looked through the book until she came to the registration of Stacy's birth. She carefully checked that against the birth cert-ificate Luba had given us, then removed the page from the book and put a new one in. On this new page the other official carefully hand copied the information from the papers we had brought. Both Lana and the senior official checked the information. Next she found Janalyn's original record, replaced the form, and the other woman copied the information. She made a mistake in copying it -- maybe she used the Russian spelling and not the Ukrainian, I don't know -- and had to recopy it on a new form. Lana and the senior official checked that one, too. Finally, after some searching, they found Lydia's original record and replaced it. After Lana and the senior official read that entry very carefully, they destroyed the original records. I asked if we could keep the original birth certificates. The senior official said that they had to be destroyed but we could make copies of them when they copied our marriage certificate.

The only copy machine in Alexandria was in the bank, which was closed that day. The senior official called a bank official and asked him to come open the bank. We gave the assistant enough money for all the copies, and the she went to the bank while we visited with the senior official and her daughter. About an hour later we had the copies. We thanked them, gave them some chocolates and a bottle of champagne, and were on our way back home. I relaxed in the back seat, a victory won.

Although it was late in the day when we arrived in Kirovograd, we went directly to the office that issues passports. They had told us that it would take about two hours to prepare the passports. Lana and I hoped that if we got the paperwork to them that evening, we would be able to pick the passports up the next morning, and be on our way to Kiev the morning after. The person we had talked with before said the passports had to be issued by another division. We went downstairs and talked to a woman at a desk in the doorway, blocking the entrance to the small office behind her. She carefully examined the paperwork, growing more tense as she read, then suddenly stood up and stalked away. Several minutes later she returned and said, "I cannot issue passports to these children. The mother is an American but the children are Ukrainian. An American cannot take Ukrainian children out of the country."

Lana explained that they were my children, that I was legally their mother.

"But they are Ukrainian citizens," the woman insisted.

Lana seemed to sense that it would not be a good idea to push any farther with this woman. We nodded and left.

As soon as we were out of the office, I started shouting at Lana.

"How could they do that? They promised that it would be a simple process. They can't just change their minds. This is really, really stupid. I just want to take my children and go home. I have no intention of spending the rest of my life in Ukraine, or of leaving my daughters behind."

Lana tried to hurry me out of the area. I was embarrassing her by yelling at her in public. Even while I was shouting at her, I knew that it was not her fault, that she had been working hard and making all sorts of sacrifices for me for months and that I was being totally unreasonable, but I couldn't seem to stop myself. In the middle of the street, I shouted at her about how stupid all these rules and all these people were, and how I just wanted to get out of this horrible place and go home.

Lana was exasperated, too, and just looked at me and said, "Don't talk to me that way. It isn't my fault."

I immediately apologized for shouting at her, especially in the middle of a downtown street. I am surprised Lana continued working so hard for me.

The girls ran to greet us as we walked into the door. Lana and I were less strict than Lana's mother. We gave them more snacks and let them be noisy and run around in the apartment.

That night, as soon as I started the bath water, Lydia climbed into the tub. She loved the water and wanted to spend all her time in the bathtub. Janalyn climbed in quickly, too. I helped them wash, then told them it was time to get out. Janalyn started crying and yelling something. I could not understand what she wanted, so I had Anna come and talk to her.

She said, "Janalyn wanted her hair washed with that shampoo that didn't sting."

I asked Anna to explain that we couldn't wash her hair every night. We would run out of shampoo too soon. Janalyn wasn't about to give up that easily and fought me as I pulled her out of the tub and dried her off. She would not stop crying. Finally Sergei took her on his lap and talked to her for a while, and she calmed down.

The next day, Lana enlisted Sergei's help. He visited several offices around town. When we went to the passport office, Lana told me, "Sit here, and don't attract attention to yourself. Don't pay any attention to the men over there."

I glanced in the direction of the men I was not supposed to pay attention to. They were sitting in a large, black Mercedes, wore nicely tailored suits, and they seemed to be watching us pretty closely. I had the uneasy feeling we were treading awfully close to Mafia territory. I sat on the edge of a brick planter, studiously ignoring the men. Sergei came, then left, then came back again. Lana finally came out and took me down the street. We stopped at a little café and had something to eat. That was the only time I went to a café in Ukraine with Lana. By the end of the day, Sergei said that the passport office could have the passports prepared by Monday if we brought in several other documents as soon as possible.

We got up early Friday and started making the rounds of various offices. In the first office, a stout, red-faced man squeezed himself behind a desk that was not as wide as he was. Lana explained why we were there. He invited us into his inner office and asked us to sit at his conference table. Lana talked a while, but as she talked I could see that she was becoming flustered. Is he refusing to help us? Lana stood and motioned for me to come. The man stood in front of the door. Lana took my hand and pushed me in front of her as we squeezed past the man and out of the office.

"He said he would give me the papers if I slept with him," Lana whispered as soon as we were out of the office. She called Sergei, and he and a couple of friends came down to talk with the man. Later that day, we were able to pick up the documents we needed from his assistant. Our experience at the three other offices we visited that day was better.

By 4:30 that evening we sat in the outer office of the Regional Governor, waiting for him to finish a meeting. After the meeting he very cordially invited us into the conference room, and we explained what we needed. We talked with him for about an hour and a half about the plight of orphans in the region, the process we had been through, and our experiences in Kirovograd. I showed him some photographs of our house, family, and friends in New Mexico. He was glad to sign the necessary papers for us and asked his assistant to start preparing them. It was after six when we got home that evening, but we felt we had achieved another victory.

We spent that entire weekend inside the apartment. Lydia refused to get more than about three feet from me, even when I went to the bathroom and most of the time she wanted to be carried. Janalyn was jealous and hit or pinched Lydia every chance she got. When I punished Janalyn, she would run to Lana for comfort and was growing closer to Lana than to me. Stacy wanted Sergei to herself whenever he was there. She could sit on his lap and charm him into playing with her for hours.

Lana kept bowls of fruit in the TV room, and the girls ate almost constantly. I was kept busy picking up tangerine and banana peels and apple cores from the floor. They drank cup after cup of weak tea and make hundreds of visits to the bathroom. Because they had been on a very regulated bathroom schedule at the orphanage, and because their schedule had been disrupted, neither Janalyn nor Lydia was reliably potty trained. I put pullups on Lydia, but Janalyn visited the bathroom at least twenty times during the day and between nine and thirteen times at night.

Monday morning, Lana left me alone with the girls while she went to the Governor's office and picked up the document he had signed, then took it to the passport office. About an hour later she charged into the apartment.

"They said they needed a few more documents, then they would send everything to the City Council, and if the City Council approved it, it would go to a special commission, and if the special commission approved it we would get the passports." Lana exclaimed. She called Svetlana and Sergei, then left again to try to obtain the rest of the documents and deliver them to the passport office. I was too distraught about the prolonged delays to say anything.

After Lana left, Janalyn hit Lydia. I spanked Janalyn and made her sit on a stool in the hallway. Then I felt really bad. How was spanking going to teach her not to hit her sister? I went into the kitchen and started crying. Anna came in and asked me what was the matter. I told her I just wanted to go home. She nodded and took care of the girls in the other room. Before long, Lydia came into the kitchen and climbed on my lap. She held my face between her hands and rubbed my nose with her nose, then hugged me and snuggled into my lap while I cried. If I did not leave Ukraine soon, I would be too depressed to take proper care of the girls. As my tears subsided I began praying, begging God to let us go home soon.

I was still sitting in the kitchen, cuddling Lydia and praying desperately, when Lana came home.

"They are preparing the passports now," she cried. "Svetlana called the passport office. She also had people of the same rank from other regions call them, as well as people from the Foreign Affairs office in Kiev, saying you could take the girls. Once the passport office knew other people had issued passports for adopted children and not gotten in trouble, they were willing to act."

Suddenly, I was in motion, sorting clothes, and deciding what needed to be packed on top for easy access, and what could be packed away.

We picked up the passports first thing in the morning while Lana's mother once again stayed with the girls. I showed them my passport and signed several papers. I have no idea what they said. Lana just said sign, and I signed. We got the passports and practically ran back to Lana's house. She called Svetlana while I packed. Svetlana asked Lana to come to Kiev as interpreter because all her usual interpreters were busy with other couples who had come to Kiev to adopt. I was extremely grateful to Lana for coming. I would have the security of working with an interpreter I knew and trusted, and she was also willing to help with the girls. Svetlana dispatched a driver to pick all of us up in Kirovograd.

I did not sleep much that night. It was Lydia's turn to sleep with me, and I was both excited about going home and nervous about the bureaucracy in Kiev. If the regional red tape had been horrendous, what would the national bureaucracy be? We were up at 5:00 a.m., ready to go. Lana packed several bags of snacks, and we fed the girls some breakfast. When the driver arrived, we fed him and filled his thermos with coffee. Then Lana got in the front seat with the driver, and I sat in the back with the girls. Lydia clung to me, whimpering, but did not cry this time. I was glad because this driver was less understanding toward the girls than our usual Kirovograd driver or Misha had been.

I was glad to be going home, but also a little frightened. There were still so many things that had to be done before we actually arrived back in New Mexico, and I wouldn't have Lana and Svetlana to take care of it for me. I would have to do all the rest of the work with the girls in tow. We had managed to do what God had sent us to Ukraine to do, but this was just the beginning, not the end. How would I handle everyday life now that everyday life would be so different from what it had been?

The answer? With God's help.

Chapter 33

"Leave your country and your people," God said, *"and go to the land I will show you."* Acts 7:3

Janalyn really needed to go to the bathroom. She told Lana, and Lana told the driver to pull off the road, got out the little pot, and let her go. About fifteen minutes later she needed to go again. The driver wasn't happy that she needed to go to the bathroom so often. She couldn't help it. This always happened when she was nervous. She managed to wait about forty-five minutes before needing to go again. She had to stop five times altogether. Then, when they started driving among lots of houses with lots of cars all around the driver said he would not stop anymore, so nobody better need to go to the bathroom. She held it in, but the stress made her feel sick. She didn't want to get in trouble for throwing up in the man's nice car. Very quietly, trying not to call attention to herself, she threw up her entire breakfast and all the snacks they had given her since leaving Kirovograd. The mess ran down her pretty green corduroy rompers.

She tried not to let anyone know, but Mama saw what had happened. Mama didn't yell, though. She said "Lana, can you take Lydia. Janalyn threw up and I need to clean her up."

Mama tried to hand Lydia to Lana, but Lydia started screaming.

The driver said, "Shut that girl up. I can't drive with her screaming like that."

Finally Mama pushed Lydia next to Stacy and had Stacy hold her while she helped Janalyn take off the pretty green corduroy romper she liked so much. Mama wrapped Janalyn in a blanket, stuffed the romper into a plastic bag and cleaned Janalyn and the car up the best she could with the damp wash cloths that had been in the bag. Janalyn sat, crying quietly, because everybody was mad at her.

They drove through the big city, crossed a bridge, and stopped at Svetlana's apartment. The driver went to get Svetlana while they stayed in the car.

It had been a really long car ride. Stacy was very tired. She was ready to get out and run around. She had eaten too much sausage, bread, apples, and cold pizza. When Janalyn vomited all over herself, Stacy had almost vomited, too.

They were in a big city now. Even Kirovograd didn't have as many houses or cars or tall buildings. Outside a big apartment building Svetlana talked with them. "You will be staying with *Baba* Ruth and *Tata* David," she told them. "They are my parents. All the places I usually have people stay are occupied right now." They didn't even get out of the car before they were driving again.

On either side of the road Stacy saw stones standing up. She asked Lana, "What are those stones?"

Lana answered, "Grave markers. This is a cemetery."

"Like where Pavlik is?" she asked.

"Yes, Pavlik is in a cemetery."

"Will people drive on top of Pavlik?"

"No," answered Lana. "We are not driving on top of anybody. They are only buried beside the road, not under it. And the cemetery where Pavlik is doesn't even have a road through it. Nobody will drive on Pavlik. They buried his body in the cemetery, but Pavlik is in heaven with God."

Stacy had no idea how Pavlik could have gotten out of the dirt to get to heaven. She had heard that heaven was a very nice place up in the sky, but she didn't know dead people went there. She thought about that until they got to the apartment where they would be staying.

This apartment building was different from the ones where Lana and Svetlana lived. It wasn't as tall, and it was not all concrete. The steps and balcony rails and several other things were wood. The trees in the yard were bigger, too. It seemed like a nice place to Stacy.

Svetlana's *Baba* and *Tata* were nice old people. *Baba* fixed dinner for them but Stacy had eaten so much on the way there that she couldn't eat any more. They would sleep in a room at the end of the hall. They watched *Dallas* on the TV that night and Stacy told everyone she would be going to Dallas, soon. Lana told her they wouldn't. Then Lana talked to Mama. Mama said they would go through Dallas, but Dallas was not their home.

The telephone rang. Stacy and Janalyn ran to listen as *Baba* talked on the phone. It was Svetlana, and *Baba* let Stacy and Janalyn talk to her. Stacy had never talked on the phone before. It was really fun. After that, every time the phone rang Stacy and Janalyn ran to see who could be the first to answer it. They got to talk with Misha, Svetlana's brother and even a couple of neighbors.

Then Papa called. Stacy could hardly wait while Mama talked with him for the longest time about when they would come and where they would meet and all sorts of boring things. She liked listening to Mama, now that she could understand some of the things she said. She knew she would learn this new language very fast.

Finally Mama let Stacy talk with him. She said, in English, "Hello Papa. We come soon there. You like?"

"I would like that very much," Papa said. "I can hardly wait to see you."

"I love you," Stacy said.

"I love you, too." Papa told her.

"You talk to sisters?" she asked.

"Yes, let me say hello to your sisters."

After he said hello to Janalyn and Lydia. Stacy wanted to talk with him some more but Mama said no. Sometimes this Mama just wasn't any fun. Papa was a lot more fun, but he was not here. He was on the other end of the telephone.

Chapter 34

Go in peace. Your journey had the Lord's approval. Judges 18:6

I was relieved to not be Svetlana's biggest problem for once. First, we had to get all the documents approved by the Ukrainian Office of Foreign Affairs. The timing was very important in this process, Misha told us.

"The papers must be turned in between 8:00 and 10:00 a.m. There is always a long line to turn in all sorts of papers for approval, and anyone who doesn't get to the front of the line by ten o'clock has to come back the next day they are open."

Misha and a friend came to pick us up at 7:00 in the morning. The girls had to go because they had to be present when we went to the consulate later in the day. As we were driving downtown, Janalyn saw a big Christmas tree, lit with bright lights and tinsel.

"*Divitis'd*" she cried excitedly, jumping up and down in her seat. As we passed, she got up on her knees and watched the tree out the back window until it disappeared from view.

Misha found a parking space about a block and a half from the Office of Foreign affairs.

"We will go stand in line," he explained. "You wait here. I will send my friend back for you when I get close to the front."

For almost an hour and a half Lana and I sat in the car with the girls. We played games, told them the English word for everything we could see from the car, and talked about the people who walked by on the sidewalk. Stacy already understood many English words. Lydia seemed to understand much of what I said, but Janalyn didn't seem to get any of it. After a while we got out and walked up and down the street a little to keep the girls occupied.

Misha's friend finally came. I followed him up the street and around a corner. As we approached the building, I saw a line extending out the door, down the block, and around the corner. We pushed through the doors. Inside the line extended across a large, high ceiling, marble lobby to a set of three desks. Misha was about three people from the front when we joined him. We were among the last people to turn our papers in that day. All the other people in the line were turned away. The line would reopen when they had processed all the papers that had been turned in that day. There was no official word on when that would be.

The girls were excited to be on our way again, especially when we passed by the Christmas tree. Our next stop was the American Consulate to get their approval of the documents. Papers had to be turned in there between 1:00 p.m. and 3:00 p.m. We played in a park across from the Consulate then ate the sandwiches Svetlana's mother had packed for us. Members of the International Community in Kiev filled the park, young children playing, mothers and grandmothers pushing strollers and teenagers out looking for some kind of activity to occupy their time until winter break was over. The girls were much braver here than they had been previously, walking as much as twenty feet away from us before coming back. Janalyn even fed part of her sandwich to a dog.

Svetlana joined us in the park just before the consulate opened. She would be able to go into the consulate, because they knew her, but everyone else would have to wait outside. We left the girl's backpacks, and Svetlana's purse with Misha and Lana to speed up the security search in the Consulate.

Because the girls were Ukrainians, we had to go through the line for

Ukrainian citizens rather than the much faster one for Americans. While we waited, the girls charmed everyone, even though they would not stay in line with me and kept running all over the small waiting room. When we finally got to the window, Stacy announced, "This is my Mama. I am going to America to live with her."

For me, it was a relief to get to the front of a line, hand someone my paperwork, explain what I wanted, and have them smile at me and say, "I'll be right back."

We had to wait a little while as the Consul read the papers, then he came out and talked with us. He recommended that we get an official seal on the adoption decree and birth certificates that guaranteed them as official documents. We were happy to do that, even though it cost fifty dollars. Then we were ready to go back to Svetlana's parents and relax. Praise God! Not a single person had said they could not process our papers.

That evening, I tried to wash some of the girl's clothes, but Svetlana's mother took over and had them all clean and pressed by morning. She gave us a delicious meal of soup, mashed potatoes and cutlets that evening, and had more breakfast than we could possibly eat the next morning.

Our first stop the next morning was at the Lot Airlines office to buy tickets to Warsaw. We had been able to buy tickets from Warsaw to Albuquerque before we left for Ukraine, but tickets from Kiev to Warsaw could not be changed or returned, so we had to wait until we knew exactly when we would be leaving. By now, Robert had paid off our remaining credit card, so I could buy the tickets.

There was no line. The person at the counter spoke English. I said, "I would like tickets for one adult and three children to Warsaw on Saturday's afternoon flight."

The clerk typed the request into her computer, swiped the credit card, and the process went without a hitch. I double and triple checked everything because I couldn't believe that, for once, things could happen without delays, arguments, and inconveniences.

The Christmas tree excited Janalyn so much that Misha drove by it whenever he could. She got just as excited every time. We saw that tree about ten times before we left Kiev.

Stacy saw a church and asked what that was. Lana told her it was where people went to worship God. She begged to stop and see Pavlik. Lana tried to explain that both Pavlik and God were in heaven and that the church was just a place where people went to talk with God. She really didn't understand it. There had been no official religious training in the orphanage. When we saw another church, she asked if that was a different God's house. When Lana told her it was the same God, she couldn't figure out why one God needed two houses. She thought about that the rest of the afternoon.

I still owed Lana for three weeks of room and board. We stopped at a hotel so I could get a cash advance to pay her. Svetlana, Stacy, and I went into the hotel to get the cash. At first the person at the Western Union booth mistook the date on the card that said "Member since" for the expiration date and told me the card was expired. Then she had trouble with the conversion rates until I told her we wanted the cash advance in dollars. She called a supervisor to come help her. Because it was taking so long to get the cash, Svetlana took Stacy into the empty bar near the Western Union booth and bought her a soda. Back in the car Stacy told everyone that she and Svetlana had gone drinking in a bar.

Our final stop of the day was at the Center for International Adoptions. When we arrived, they had champagne and chocolates waiting. We drank toasts all around. They even poured a little champagne for Stacy and Janalyn. They congratulated us on completing the adoption and gave us some final papers we needed. We drove back to the Office of International Affairs and left Svetlana to pick up our stamped and approved documents, then to the train station.

We said a tearful good-by to Lana as she took the train back to Kirovograd. Janalyn clung to her, begging to go with her. She was obviously frightened of being left in the care of someone whose words she did not understand and who was taking her off to a strange place. She could understand Lana and loved Lana. With me she felt like just an extra kid.

Chapter 35

The heavens declare the glory of God, the skies proclaim the work of his hands.
Psalm 19:1

Janalyn had no one to tell her what Mama was saying except Stacy, and she really didn't trust Stacy to tell the truth. Stacy had a way of making things go her way, even if she had to tell lies. Lana had told her they would spend one more night with *Baba* and *Tata,* then go to the airport. She stayed very close to *Baba* that night and let Stacy and Lydia be with Mama. She wasn't too sure how to behave with Mama.

The morning after Lana left, Misha and Svetlana took them to the airport. There was a new person there to tell them what Mama said. Mama seemed to know him. His name was Yuri. Stacy said Papa would meet them at another airport, after they had flown in an airplane.

Mama gave Misha, Svetlana, and Yuri some gifts in the car. Janalyn wished she had some gifts to open. Misha bought Janalyn and Stacy each a whole pack of gum once they got to the airport. Yuri helped Mama with the big suitcase. They even let him come to the check-in place, but Misha and Svetlana had to stay outside the little fence. Janalyn and Stacy were carrying their backpacks. They had packed them with their favorite toys and books before they left. After the man took the big suitcase away everyone hugged and kissed Misha, Svetlana, and Yuri good-bye. They all stood at the fence and watched Janalyn, Stacy, Mama and Lydia go on the moving stairs. Even after they gave the man the big suitcases, Mama still carried a bag with some of her stuff in it, a bag for Lydia, her purse, a big plastic bag of food *Baba* had packed and Lydia. She couldn't even hold Janalyn's hand. Mama pushed

Stacy onto the moving stairs. She tried to push Janalyn but Janalyn panicked. She turned around and ran off just as Mama stepped on. Janalyn stood at the bottom staring after them as they disappeared. A nice man in a pretty blue uniform with wings on the front took her hand and led her onto the moving stairs. He called them an escalator. He picked her up and carried her up the escalator to Mama.

At the top of the escalators were five desks with uniformed men behind them. Mama got in one line and waited, even though it was the slowest line. Other people switched back and forth between lines, but Mama just stood in the same line and moved slowly forward. Stacy kept begging her to get in a different line, but she wouldn't. They finally got the front of the line. Mama showed all sorts of papers to the man. He asked her for something else, and she couldn't find it. Mama put Lydia down and searched through her purse and bag. Lydia was crying because she wanted to be carried, Stacy was wandering off because she was ready to go. Janalyn was looking for the nice man who had helped her up the escalator. Finally the man said Mama could go even though she never found the paper he wanted.

They sat on some chairs, and Mama gave them the apples *Baba* had packed for the trip. Janalyn took one bite out of her apple and realized she had to go to the bathroom. Mama under-stood when she asked but wasn't moving very fast. She picked up all the carry-on luggage, arranged it over her shoulders and arms, then picked up Lydia and finally they headed for the bathroom. A nice lady in an apron watched Mama's luggage and Lydia while Mama helped Janalyn use the big toilet. Lydia didn't like toilets. She refused to go past the door, so the lady had to stand outside to watch her. While Mama helped Janalyn, Stacy finished and headed out of the bathroom. The attendant stopped her and made her wait. Mama gave her all the Ukrainian money she had left.

When they came out of the bathroom, the seats they had been sitting in were taken. They found different seats, but they could not see the place where people got on the airplanes from these seats. Somebody kept making announcements on the speakers in the ceiling. Janalyn thought they were talking in Ukrainian and Russian, plus a couple of other languages, but she could not understand any of it. Every time they said something though, Mama got up to look around the corner. Lydia and Janalyn played with their toys until the woman who had been standing by the gate came to get them. Janalyn did not know why Mama had been so worried when this nice lady was there to look after them.

At the gate Mama had to show the people all those papers again, then they walked down a ramp, down some stairs, and across the blacktop to a bus. Mama carried Lydia and the carry-on bags, but managed to get one hand free to hold Janalyn's hand. Janalyn was very grateful because she was sure she would have fallen down if Mama hadn't taken her hand. There were people crowding all around them and pushing Mama from behind. Janalyn would probably have been trampled if she had fallen. This was the most frightening thing that had ever happened to her. Stacy grabbed Mama's coat and followed behind them. She seemed a little scared, too.

On the bus Mama showed Janalyn and Stacy how to hold onto a bar and put her leg against their backs so they would not fall. She wrapped one arm around the bar above their heads so she wouldn't fall and carried all the bags, and Lydia, in the other. When the bus started to move, Lydia started screaming, which scared Janalyn who started crying, too. When the bus stopped, people around them scurried off. Mama went down the steps of the bus and lifted Janalyn down with one arm then held Stacy's hand while she climbed down. Janalyn looked at the steep stairs of the plane. There was no way she was going up there.

Just then a nice *Baba* and *Tata* came along. The man picked up Janalyn and carried her up the steps while the woman held Stacy's hand. When they got on the plane, Mama found a row of seats for them. Janalyn got to sit by a window. She could see the men loading the suitcases into the plane. Lydia was in the middle between Janalyn and Mama. Stacy was on the other side of the aisle. Stacy was talking with the people sitting next to her, probably telling them she was going to America. Janalyn stared out the window at the men below.

She wondered how Lydia would behave when they took off. Mama sure put up with a lot of crying from her. Janalyn would have slapped her a long time ago. Mama didn't put the seatbelt on Lydia until the plane started going. Lydia was too busy fighting the seatbelt to notice that the plane was moving. As they climbed out of the clouds, the bright yellow sun made everything glow. Janalyn gasped. She looked at Mama. Mama's smile glowed just like the sun. Now she knew she could love Mama. Mama liked beautiful things, too.

Chapter 36

I will put my trust in Him. Here am I and the children the Lord has given me.
Isaiah 8: 17b, 18a

The older couple helped us get off the plane, took a different hallway after deplaning. I think they were Polish and had to go to a different customs line. The man who had been sitting next to Stacy helped us down the steps and through the hallways to the Immigration desk. There were several desks with turnstiles at the entrance to a large room where we would pick up our luggage.

Our flight was scheduled to arrive at 3:30 that afternoon. Robert was scheduled to arrive from the United States at 3:00. He planned to wait for us in the customs area so we could go through customs and to the hotel together. Friends in the United States said he was crazy to expect that we would both actually arrive in customs at the same time. He just told them to pray for us. When we got to the turnstiles Stacy saw Robert. He had already collected our luggage and put it on a cart with his.

Stacy ducked under the barrier and tried to run to Robert. One of the Immigration officials held her back, and she returned to my side. I had to hold onto her the entire time the Immigration Official was examining our passports, visas, adoption papers, and other information. They looked at the adoption decree, then had to find someone who could read English or Ukrainian so they could verify it was what I said it was. At last they let us go through the turnstile to Robert. He looked so fresh and happy, even after a trans-Atlantic flight that I almost collapsed in his arms. Customs was a fast, simple process since the only thing of any value we had acquired in Ukraine

242

was children.

We changed some money into Polish *złotys* and Robert found a taxi driver who would take us to the Marriott for what we had been told was a reasonable fare. There were several taxi drivers who offered to take us for their "special American price."

On the way to the hotel Stacy chattered to the taxi driver in what we presume was Russian, since he could understand her, although he may have understood Ukrainian, too. He tried to be professional and keep his eyes on the road, but she soon had him laughing at her jokes.

At the hotel I lay on the bed as soon as the bellhop left. Robert lay down beside me and tried to talk, but Lydia would have none of that. She tried to climb up on the bed, which was too tall for her, so she started crying. I lifted her up onto the bed, and she lay between Robert and me.

After a while, I examined what was in the refrigerator and decided to have a drink of ice water. I gave Janalyn the ice bucket and Stacy the key card. Taking Lydia's hand we set off on an expedition to find ice. It wasn't far from our room, but we went the long way, all the way around that floor of the hotel. We walked at Lydia's pace, except when Janalyn stopped to admire the copies of paintings by old Masters on the walls. Janalyn wanted to examine them much longer than Lydia or Stacy could tolerate. At the ice machine I put a scoop of ice in the bucket.

"What is that?" asked Stacy.

"Ice," I said, and let them lick it.

They stared at me with wide eyes. They had seen ice on the walkways at the orphanage and icicles hanging from the roof, but never ice in a big metal machine inside a building. We returned to our room, and I showed Stacy how to open the door. She suddenly became the expert at door opening. I put some of the ice in a glass, and they watched it melt. They really didn't like to drink ice water, but it was fascinating to put ice in a glass and watch it melt. Before long they wanted to get more ice from the machine.

We went for an early dinner at the hotel restaurant. Our bodies were still on Ukrainian time, which is two hours later than Polish time. Robert's body had no idea what time it was, but he can eat any time. We ordered things like *borscht* and potatoes for the girls. Robert ordered beef burgundy, but I chose a trip to the salad bar and seafood buffet. The girls went with me and discovered the wonders of a salad bar. They still love to eat at salad bars.

Despite the fact that we were almost the only ones in the restaurant, it took almost an hour and a half for the meal to be served and eaten. During this time, of course, we had to make several trips to the bathroom. On her second trip to the bathroom Janalyn discovered an eight-foot square still life on one wall. After we ate, she and I sat on the bench across from that still life for almost half an hour, examining every piece of it and commenting on different parts while Robert took the other girls for rides on the escalators.

The escalators became our main form of entertainment at the hotel. We tried to find the least used escalators in the hotel and ride those. In the morning, we rode from the ballrooms to the meeting rooms. In the evening, we went from the shops to the offices. Once the girls learned the trick of opening the doors, they fought to be the one to unlock the door or push the buttons on the elevator. We allowed one to push the call button for the elevator, one to push the button inside, and one to open the door each time we came or went.

That night we put the three girls in one queen-sized bed, and Robert and

I slept in the other. In the middle of the night Lydia got up and wanted to sleep with us. Stacy had flung herself sideways across the bed and Janalyn was sleeping at right angles to her so there was no place left for Lydia. I pulled Lydia into bed with us, but didn't get much sleep the rest of the night because she kept kicking me. If I moved away from her, Robert rolled over on top of me. I was more tired in the morning than I had been when I went to bed.

We ordered breakfast from room service. It was expensive, but we didn't have to wait in the restaurant for it. Health certificates were required before they could enter the United States and only doctors certified by the Embassy could give the exams. The doctor ICA recommended agreed to give the girls exams on Sunday. We got there a little early and her housekeeper let us in, leaving some toys to play with.

The girls could never seem to play for very long without shouting and fighting. Stacy and Janalyn resented our interference with their fights. When we insisted that they let Lydia play with the toy she had picked up first, rather then grabbing it out of her hands, they frowned at us and threw their toys against the wall. The doctor walked in during all this and seemed to think we did not have adequate control of the girls. She immediately ordered them to be quiet and put the toys away. "You must obey your parents," she told them in Russian.

She examined Stacy first.

"Walk over to that wall," she told her. Stacy walked there and back.

"Make a little house with these blocks," she told her. Stacy complied.

She handed her a toy. "Put the rings on the stick in order from largest to smallest." That was no problem for Stacy.

She repeated the process with Janalyn and Lydia, then examined their medical records. She declared they were in excellent health, although she said Janalyn was slightly delayed and Lydia somewhat more delayed in physical development. She felt confident that with proper care they would catch up. The form required by US immigrations includes an immunization record. Both Janalyn and Stacy had records of ten polio immunizations, and Lydia had seven. She listed them across the page even though the American form did not have space for that many. She said she could not understand why they had received so many immunizations.

After the examination the doctor had to prepare more paperwork to be taken to the Embassy. Rather than wait at the doctor's office, we returned to the hotel and spent the rest of the day watching television. The girls could not understand why we would not let them watch certain shows. They thought a steamy romance, or even the pornographic channels, which we quickly blocked out, were as good as anything else.

Their entry permits required passport photos taken to U.S. specifications. In the early afternoon we decided to get those and to get some lunch. The hotel concierge told us there was a photo shop two blocks up the street from the hotel. Robert walked with Stacy and Janalyn while Lydia rode on my back in a backpack carrier. It was too big for me, and rubbed my hips as well as my shoulders, so we transferred it to Robert. The only way Lydia would tolerate that was if I walked along beside her and held her hand. When we got to the photo shop, it was closed.

We stood by the door asking each other "What do we do now," when someone came up to us and said in excellent English, "There is another photo shop in the underground mall." He had obviously heard us talking and understood our dilemma. Across the street from the hotel was an entrance to the underground mall. This was a series of tunnels that led to the trains, but it was lined with shops of various kinds.

As we walked back the way we had come, Stacy kept saying, "We are hungry. We need to eat."

The first restaurant we came to was McDonald's. We had vowed we would wait a long time before we took the girls to McDonald's, but we did not want to wait an hour for the other restaurants to open, so we bought them their first Big Macs. Janalyn ate the french fries and the bun. The other girls would only eat Chicken McNuggets, and we had to take the breading off the outside before they would do that.

We found the passport photo shop a little farther along. The photographer was on an errand and only the film sales clerk was there. She asked us to come back later. For about an hour, we walked through the underground mall looking at other shops and interesting sights. When we returned to the passport photo shop, the photographer was still not there. The clerk finally agreed to take the pictures.

Stacy sat on the little stool. The requirements for U.S. passport photos were different from the Polish requirements. Robert tilted her head slightly.

"She should be looking at me," the clerk said.

"No, her right ear needs to be showing." He showed her the requirements.

She got a perfect picture of Stacy on the first try. Then Janalyn sat. Her picture was just right, too. When we put Lydia on the stool, she refused to stay there. I held her on the stool but she refused to look at the camera. If Robert, Stacy, or Janalyn tried to get her to look at them, she made faces.

Other customers were waiting, and the clerk was getting frustrated. Finally, one of the other customers held up a bear for her to look at while I held her head from behind, trying not to let my hand show. Her picture looks like a mug shot, but it was good enough for the Embassy to accept.

Late in the afternoon Robert went to get the documents from the doctor while we sat in the hotel room watching television and melting more ice. He brought snacks back from a little shop down the street for us to eat that night.

We had planned to go to the US Embassy first thing Monday morning, but it turned out it was Martin Luther King's birthday. We thought there had been too many holidays in Ukraine, but the American Embassy in Warsaw closes for both Polish and American holidays'. Robert was delighted by this turn of events because he really wanted to do some sightseeing. We got a taxi and went to old Warsaw. First we toured in a horse drawn carriage, which was a wonderful way for Robert to see the buildings and the girls to stay interested without getting too tired. After the carriage ride we walked around a while and looked at shops and art displays in the open square.

It was very cold, but sunny and there were several artists displaying their work. Lydia would not walk, nor would she let Robert carry her. Before long I was not thinking of much besides the pain in my feet from walking on cold cobblestones in thin-soled shoes and the pain in my back from carrying Lydia. I wished I still had Lana's fur lined boots. Janalyn enjoyed looking at the art and chasing birds. Stacy enjoyed talking with everyone she met, and Robert enjoyed taking pictures of anything and everything. Finally he asked me what I wanted to do.

"Sit down and eat," I said.

Our guide on the carriage ride had told us about a wonderful little Polish family restaurant that he recommended. We walked back the way we thought we had come on the carriage ride, looking for the restaurant, but we couldn't find it. After we had walked a while, the girls started whining and complaining. I said to Robert, "Let's give up on finding that place he recommended and just go to the next place we see."

He agreed, and the next place we saw was Pizza Hut. We ordered a pizza and salad. The girls ate the salad but didn't really go for the pizza. The pizza Lana had made for them had very thick crust and very little tomato sauce. This pizza had thin crust and lots of tomato sauce. We took the leftover pizza back to the hotel and saved it for a midnight snack for Robert and me.

Our appointment at the embassy was at 9:00 in the morning. We got a taxi for the one-mile ride to the embassy, knowing it would take the girls a long time to walk that distance. In front of the embassy were three lines, one for US citizens, one for Eastern Europeans applying for visas, and the third for everyone else. We got in the line for American citizens, which fortunately had about fifty fewer people than the other line. They started admitting that line into the embassy first, too, so it didn't take long for us to get inside. Once inside, we registered that we were there and went into the waiting room for people applying for visas. This was a large, undecorated room with row upon row of dark colored plastic chairs. The walls were painted the same institutional green used around the world for such rooms. Everyone waited in the chairs until an Embassy official called their name. Apparently they called the names in the order of the appointments, but a 9:00 appointment did not mean your name was called at 9:00.

ICA had sent us a six-page form to fill out at the Embassy. We started filling it out while we waited. It was a new form that ICA didn't have experience with. We worked on the form for about forty-five minutes before we were called up to the window to submit a preliminary request and see that our paperwork was in order. At the window the official said that the regulations had changed and Robert and I each needed to fill out a form for each of the girls. Thus we had to fill out six six-page forms before we could proceed. The form was supposed to prove our ability to support the children. Our tax returns and the letter from our accountant were in the packet already prepared for them, but we still had to fill out this other form.

As we stood at the counter filling out the forms the girls whined, complained, fought, and demanded to go to the bathroom about four times. Most of the people working in this office were Polish citizens, who were pleasant and helpful but still had the Soviet mind set about long lines. They were in no hurry to process anything just because many people were waiting. When we had finally finished the forms, they told us we had to go to the other part of the embassy to get them notarized.

About twenty Americans waited in the other room to get their passports renewed or deal with other business. This room was pleasant, with upholstered wooden chairs around the perimeter and an interesting patterned tile floor. The person who could notarize our papers was busy with someone else, so we had to sit and wait for about an hour and a half. We got acquainted with an American missionary family who were there from Ukraine to get their passports renewed. We were having a really good visit with the parents while their children played with the girls.

Lydia ran across the room to get away from their daughter in a game of pretend monster and fell on the tile floor. We could hear a crack as her head hit the floor and a big goose egg began to rise almost immediately. As soon as I picked her up, she howled in pain. Everyone in the waiting room was concerned for her and offered suggestions on how to calm her. I sent Robert to the restroom and to get some wet paper towels, but there were no paper towels in the bathroom, so I just held her while she cried. A man gave us his watch to hold on her head, because the metal was cold. I tried that and it seemed to calm her a bit. The rest of the day she would not let go of me, and I had to do all our business with Lydia either clinging to my neck or sitting on the counter in front of me. We finally got our notarizations and went back to the other room to wait some more.

We had thought the whole process would take about two hours, so we had not brought anything to eat. Robert had enough Polish coins for one grape soda from the vending machines in the hallway. We split it three ways among the girls. Finally, at 2:00 in the afternoon all the paperwork was in order. Then we had to pay fees. The clerk wrote the amount we owed on a little slip of paper. I sat with the girls near the bathroom, with which we were well acquainted by now, while Robert stood in the fee-paying line with our little slip of paper. Robert gave the clerk a hundred dollar bill to pay the fee.

"I can't accept this," he said.

"Why not?" Robert asked.

"It is defective. See, it has a mark on it right here."

Robert looked. There was a little mark from a black permanent marker on it. Robert gave the clerk another one, but he wouldn't accept it because it was too old. We didn't have any other money with us. The Immigration official had said they would have the visas ready to pick up by 5:00 p.m., although we had to be back by 4:30 p.m. because that is when they lock the doors. The clerk said we could pay when we came to pick up the visas.

So, with two hundred dollars in our pockets but lacking any money we could spend in Poland, we walked back to the hotel. It was quite a hike for the girls but they had plenty of pent-up energy from sitting all day at the Embassy. Lydia let Robert carry her part of the time, after I had made her walk about two blocks. Janalyn was starting to get excited rather than terrified when she saw a dog, provided it was a small dog and didn't get too close. It turned out to be one of the most pleasant walks we had taken in Ukraine or Poland. Robert showed Janalyn the details on different buildings, which she found as interesting as he did, and Stacy looked into all the shops and speculated about the people who worked there and the things they sold.

"Fairy store," she said.

"What makes you think that is a fairy store?" I asked.

"Pretty," she said. "Feathers and flowers."

I looked into the store, where they had a display of skirts made of sheer fabric with feathers and flowers. It did look a little like a clothing store for fairies.

All three girls were concerned about cracks in the sidewalk and refused to step on any grate, manhole cover, or anything else set into the sidewalk or street. That was a very reasonable thing for someone raised in Ukraine. Manhole covers and grates were quite likely to fall in if you stepped on them in Ukraine.

Back at the hotel, Robert got a cash advance on the credit cards, checking the bills carefully to make sure they were new and unmarked bills and returned immediately to get the visas. They gave him the girls' stamped passports and three sealed envelopes, which he was instructed not to open before we handed them to Immigration officials in the United States.

We spent another evening riding escalators, ordered dinner from room service, and watched cartoons on television. That night we made a bed for Lydia on the floor next to our bed, using our bedspread and cushions from the chairs. Everyone slept much better.

Chapter 37

You turned my wailing into dancing; you removed my sackcloth and clothed me with joy, that my heart may sing to you and not be silent. O Lord my God, I will give you thanks forever. Psalm 30:11-12

Robert is a morning person. He was anxious that we check in on time for our flight home. Our plane left at 7:00 in the morning. We arrived at the airport at 5:00 a.m.. They were just unlocking the doors. The airport was deserted.

We got a cart, loaded our piles of luggage on it, and the girls had fun pushing it around the empty airport. Before long a snack bar opened, and we bought coffee, tea, and rolls. The girls were more interested in pushing the cart around the deserted airport than in eating. More people filtered in, we made a couple of trips to the bathroom, and then the Lufthansa desk opened up. We pushed our cart over to the counter and checked in. The girls went through the security check like pros, having done this twice before. Almost immediately we boarded the plane to Frankfurt, Germany. This was a short flight, and the girls were very good, so it went quickly.

During our two hours in Frankfurt we had to get our luggage, go through an Immigration and Customs check, then go through another security check. Robert and I could have gone anywhere in the city, since we are American citizens, but the girls could not leave the security area. We sat in the waiting area and watched people until it was time to board the plane for Dallas.

Robert, Stacy and Janalyn sat in the row in front, next to a man from

Palestine. Lydia and I had the next row to ourselves. Behind us sat a child psychologist from the former East Germany. We showed the girls how to use the earphones and tuned them to some relaxing music. They promptly changed to different channels. Lydia had fought her seatbelt more vigorously on each flight and did not want it on at all on this flight. I held her in my lap until we were taxiing down the runway, then quickly strapped her in her seat. She screamed and refused to accept the handful of gummy bears I gave her in an attempt to get her to be quiet. As soon as I could, I unstrapped her. She climbed on my lap and began looking for gummy bears.

As soon as Stacy could get up, she began visiting up and down the aisles, explaining that she had been adopted and was going to America. Soon everyone on the plane knew they had just been adopted. Stacy talked with anyone who could understand Russian, and Robert talked with those who knew English.

Stacy's seat was on the right side of the plane and the rest of us were on the left. That meant that Stacy had a different stewardess. Stacy's stewardess brought a coloring book for her. That started a very physical argument between Stacy and Janalyn. While Robert and I were trying to separate them, the child psychologist went back to the flight attendant's station and got coloring books for the other two girls. Hours later the other stewardess brought hand puppets for Janalyn and Lydia. By that time Lydia was asleep, so Stacy played with Lydia's hand puppet.

After we ate, I hoped the girls would settle down and go to sleep. They were not the least bit interested in sleep. Stacy wanted to visit, and Janalyn went in search of a lap to cuddle up in. She spent most of the rest of the flight cuddled up in the laps of total strangers. Lydia wanted to walk the aisles -- holding onto me, of course.

Lydia also had diarrhea. By now we were out of pullups, but I had bought some disposable diapers. When I took her to the bathroom to change her, she was terrified. I don't know if it was her extremely sensitive sense of smell or if it was the noise of the bathroom, where the engine noise was louder than in the seating area. I managed to get the diaper off and was reaching for the wipes to clean her up, when she wiggled out of my grasp. She stood up on the changing table, took a flying leap and wrapped her arms and legs around me. I pried her loose and used most of my wipes to clean Lydia, the bathroom, and myself.

We had brought a change of clothes for the girls in the carry-on luggage, knowing they were likely to need it. Because the carry-on was full of their clothes and toys, we had not brought a change of clothes for ourselves. People eyed me suspiciously as I made my way back up the aisle. I got some perfume out of my purse and sprayed myself thoroughly. Robert turned around, looked at my damp sweater, sniffed a little, raised his eyebrows and turned back around. He was very busy trying to keep the older girls from embarrassing us too badly.

Men hardly ever came to the orphanage. There are two typical reactions among the children at the orphanage when they do see men. Either they immediately attach themselves to and adore any man they meet, or they are frightened of them. Stacy and Janalyn had the former reaction. Lydia had the latter. It was months before any man, including Robert, could pick Lydia up without a great deal of coaxing and gentleness. It was even longer before Stacy and Janalyn would learn that they could not hug and climb on the lap of any man they saw. They were soon fighting over the Palestinian man who shared the row with Robert and Stacy. He had already been up more than twenty-four hours before he got on this plane, so Robert tried to keep the girls away, but he said it was fine. He had six children, and he missed them already. When the girls were not on his lap, they were on the lap of the child psychologist or a grandfather across the aisle.

Lydia eventually went to sleep on my lap and slept fitfully for about three hours. Janalyn slept for about an hour on the empty seats beside me, after we forced her to lie down. I dozed a little, but it was difficult with Lydia squirming on my lap and Janalyn resting her head on my leg. Eventually, Robert fell asleep, and Stacy decided to come back and share the blanket and seat with Janalyn. That woke Janalyn up, and I had to move over to sit between them so one could lie on one side and one on the other, with Lydia on top of me. That woke Lydia up, but she went right back to sleep. Janalyn went back to sleep quickly, too. Stacy was almost asleep when the stewardesses bought hot towels and breakfast. We were about two hours out of Dallas. Although I hadn't really slept at all, I was so excited to be going home that I didn't feel the exhaustion.

At the Dallas airport, we gave the Immigration officer our packets, and he disappeared with them. Soon everyone from our plane was gone except a mother, her daughter, and a friend who were emigrating from Germany. The girls, including the four-year-old German girl, who was taller than Stacy, started having races in the hallway. After the German family was cleared and left for Customs, we sat in the chairs to wait. It was really taking a long time, so Robert went to ask if there was any problem. Someone went to check, and before long a supervisor came back to apologize. He said they normally try to expedite adoption cases as much as possible, but we had given our papers to a new employee who did not know the procedure for adoptions. He gave us the girls' visas, their temporary green cards, and we were free to go.

We got on the train to the terminal where we would board our final flight to Albuquerque.

"This is America," Robert said.

"America?" Stacy asked, looking out the window at the construction debris beside the train tracks.

"Yes." Robert said. "This is Dallas."

"No. Not Dallas," she said. She had seen Dallas on television and this was definitely not Dallas.

"Yes. This is Dallas."

Stacy checked the construction outside the train again and made a face. "Go home?"

"Yes. One more airplane ride, and we will be home."

"No," she said. "No more airplane."

"Just one more. For a short time." Robert assured her.

She folded her arms and pouted.

At our stop, Janalyn refused to get off the train. I was holding Lydia and one piece of carry-on luggage. Robert was pushing from behind, holding the rest of the carry on luggage and Stacy's hand. Janalyn was standing at the threshold and refusing to move. I balanced Lydia on my hip, grabbed Janalyn's hand and pulled her out of the train. She tripped, but I lifted her by one arm and pulled her aside to keep her from getting trampled. She gave me a dirty look and refused to go with me up the escalator. Robert handed me most of the carry on luggage, took Stacy by one hand and Janalyn by the other and led them up the escalator to the waiting area for our final flight. I trudged into the waiting area a little later, Lydia clinging to my neck, my purse and four pieces of carry-on luggage draped on my body.

"You watch this stuff while I go check in," Robert said when I had gotten settled into a seat. Janalyn followed him to the counter, scowling at me as they went. Stacy started down the jetway.

"Come back here, Stacy." I called. She slowed but didn't stop.

"Stacy!" I called, trying to untangle my feet from the straps of my purse and the luggage. Lydia started whining because I was bending over and that made her feel unbalanced.

Someone else went after Stacy and steered her back to me. I smiled at the woman. She seemed to understand, although other people appeared to be thinking, "Why can't this woman control her children?"

On this flight we were seated at the very back, next to the galley. Janalyn was still mad at me and insisted on sitting next to Robert. Stacy got the aisle seat, and Lydia sat with me. The flight took about an hour and a half. The flight attendants were totally charmed by the girls and brought extra juice and snacks for them. Stacy was as cute and charming as ever, even as tired as she was. Janalyn didn't get up once to go to the bathroom. Just as we were landing, Janalyn threw up everything she had eaten in the past several hours. One of the flight attendants was walking by just as she threw up. She quickly brought a plastic bag and some wipes. I reached over the seat and rolled up the skirt of Janalyn's dress. I just kept rolling until the dress was off her. We put it in a plastic bag and took it home that way. The stewardess brought some more wet wipes, and we were still cleaning when the plane landed and other people started getting off. We gathered up all our things, put the girl's coats on them as people in the two seats behind us left and finally started up the aisle.

Meanwhile, outside the plane about forty people waited with balloons, signs, noisemakers and gifts. All the other people streamed off the plane. Then people stopped coming. Our friends asked if we were really on the plane. Jaynie, Lydia's Godmother, started down the jetway just as we rounded the bend. I caught a glimpse of her as she ran back the other way shouting, "Here they come! Here they come!"

Janalyn, wearing nothing under her coat but her shirt and tights, led the way. All of us smelled as bad as I had earlier in the day. We were greeted with cheers, screams, and tears. Strangers stopped to find out what was going on and congratulated us. Ed, who had gone on the first mission trip with the church, took Lydia out of my arms, and she promptly fell asleep on his shoulder, completely without protest.

Bethany Lust, the pastor's five-year-old daughter, handed each of the girls a bag of toys. She had been very upset with her parents because they did not have any gifts to give to the girls when they arrived. She had gone through her own toys and collected a bag of toys for each of the girls.

We gradually moved toward the luggage claim area, a milling crowd with Stacy and Janalyn at the center. While we waited for our luggage, we said good-bye to a few people who had other places to be that evening. We waited some more for the luggage and still it did not come. Then there wasn't any more luggage on the carrousel. Robert and Janalyn's Godfather, Bob Prindle, went to check on it.

The man at the counter said, "Let's see. That is all of the luggage that is supposed to be on the flight. Wait. Except one set. From Frank-furt." We gave them our name and address, and they promised to deliver it later.

We were so disoriented that we had no sense of the time. It was only about 5:00 p.m. but we felt like it was very late at night. My mother, our employees, and the girl's godparents and their families came to our house. As we walked toward the parking lot, we sorted out who would ride with whom. Janalyn had immediately latched onto Bob and was not going to let him go. Lydia's car seat was in Jaynie's van, so she and I would have to go with Jaynie. Stacy could not decide which of her new friends she wanted to ride with but ended up going in the same car as Janalyn. We finally got it all sorted out and drove home. At the door we stopped for a picture of us all walking into the house for the first time.

My mother had dinner for us in the refrigerator although she and Katrina, one of our employees, had plans to go out to dinner. The girls' godparents stayed. Lydia's godfather Bob Hakeem brought some hamburgers and french fries from McDonald's for the girls, although they weren't interested in eating them. They were most interested in playing with their new friends. With eleven kids running through the house there was great joyful noise. Steve Herrera, Stacy's godfather, was a great hit as he made faces and chased them. While the kids played, Nancy, Janalyn's godmother, and Celeste, Stacy's godmother, went out and bought pajamas and underwear to replace what was in the luggage.

The girls did eat a couple of bananas and an apple each. Around 7:30 p.m. Stacy's and Lydia's godparents had to leave. Stacy cried like her heart was broken, so Janalyn's godparents stayed to help with the transition. Janalyn's godmother gave the girls a bath, and her godfather read them bedtime stories. They did not leave until the girls were in bed around 9:00

p.m. Still, when they left, Stacy cried for over an hour.

The next morning Stacy got up and asked where we were. We told her we were at home, *doma*. Her eyes got wide, and she looked around.

"*Doma*?" she cried.

Suddenly we realized that she had thought this was one more stop on our long trip home and that we would soon be leaving this house, too. She had cried the night before because this was a really fun stop with all the kids to play with, and she was afraid she would not see them again.

Several months after we got home, I asked Betsy for any pictures she had of their first trip to the orphanage to see if I could find our girls in any of them. She handed me the picture that had hung on the bulletin board for so long and there, standing beside Violetta, I recognized the girl in the blue bow, my Stacy.

Epilog

Stacy started school within two weeks of our return home. On St. Valentines Day I got her some *Anastasia* valentines to give to the other kids. The significance was not lost on many of the parents, and some of the kids understood how much Stacy's life had paralleled that of Stacy in the movie.

The day after St. Valentine's Stacy cried a lot. She asked about Pavlik, and I told her Pavlik was in Heaven. She remembered that, and a few weeks later when she could express herself a little better, she asked, "Is there somebody to take care of you in Heaven?"

"God takes very, very good care of everyone in Heaven," I told her.

"Is there food to eat in Heaven?"

"Heaven has the best food you can imagine, and lots of it."

"Even bananas?" she asked.

"Even bananas."

"Are there toys in Heaven?"

"Yes. I'm sure there are lots of toys in Heaven."

"Can kids play with them?"

"Yes. Kids can play with them."

"Heaven must be even better than America. I would like to go to Heaven."

"Not right now."

"Why not?"

"Because you would have to die first, and I don't want you to die."

"But I would get to see Pavlik and my grandfathers, wouldn't I?"

"Yes."

Several months later we watched *Touched by an Angel*. Stacy decided that if John Dye took Pavlik to Heaven he must be very well taken care of.

Stacy could make herself understood in English within three weeks and could pass for an American six year old within three months. Stacy is now a beautiful twelve year old who attends Family School, which is a program where she spends half of the day in public school and half in home school. She is still very social and very involved in both basketball and the mission efforts of the youth group at St. Stephen's United Methodist Church. She also takes voice lessons.

Janalyn took longer to start speaking English. She went through a stage in which she spoke gibberish that sounded like English. I am not sure if she thought she was speaking English or if she knew her words didn't mean anything but she wanted to sound like everyone else in the house. Janalyn has continued to love art and is very creative in the artwork she does. She continues to excel in drama and music, performs with a children's acting troupe in Albuquerque and leads singing in Children's Worship at St. Stephens. More than once people have told me, "I saw your daughter - the long-legged one." I know they mean Janalyn. She is a tall 11-year-old with two goals. One is to attend the Public Academy for Performing Arts here in Albuquerque in middle school and high school, and the other is to own a restaurant someday.

Lydia refused to be separated from me for the first three months we were home. Finally, one day Robert offered to let her ride in his pickup truck. The desire to ride in the truck overcame her need to be with me, and she went with him for the first time. She started speech and occupational therapy six months after coming home. The mother of a boy in Janalyn's drama class told us about Skyline therapy, where they offer hippotherapy (horse therapy). Lydia loved it immediately and now rides beautifully. Soon she will get her own horse. She chatters constantly, like her nine-year-old friends, and is a tease and a clown. She is as outgoing as Stacy and thrives on being the center of attention.

The adoption ended up costing more than fifty thousand dollars, and the business had lost over twenty thousand dollars through our absence. Robert started working very hard to make all that up. He was able to double the income of the business in the year following the adoption. The Federal adoption tax credits helped, and we soon had all the credit card debt paid off and had larger reserves in the bank than ever before.

It soon became apparent that the amount of time Robert was spending at work was not appropriate. He needed to adjust his schedule for being the father of three young girls. We sold one of the office buildings we had downtown so he would not have to take the time to maintain that. The next year we scaled down the business, sold the second office building, and moved his office into our home. As a result we were able to pay off all the debts we incurred from adopting the girls and are now better off financially than we ever were. We believe it is because we answered God's call to become parents to these girls, even though it was a difficult path.

A year after we adopted our girls, Yuri and Julia were adopt-ed by another couple in New Mexico. Since then more than forty other adoptions from that orphanage have been completed, all by the same judge. We have been told that a spiritual renewal has occurred in Kirovograd. Lana said it had a lot to do with our being there and exhibiting a Christian spirit of love, faith, and perseverance.

Immediately after we got home, my mother started coming over three times a week to "help out." After a few months, she was coming over every day. Then she decided that she had to drive too much and that we should sell our house and hers to build a new house with an attached apartment for her so that she could help out without all the driving. We now live in our new house, and Grandma is very much a part of the lives of the girls.

It took me months to let go of my anger over what we went through in Ukraine. Gradually I came to see the lessons Gad had taught us, and how valuable they are in everyday life. That realization, and seeing all the other families who have been made complete because we persevered through those hard times has helped. As the girls began to cling less and love more life became easier until I could relax and just love them back. My life now centers on my girls, my garden, and my writing.

Photo Credits: Betsy Castle, Robert Habiger, Lana Shandruk, and Lynn Ellen Doxon.

Rainbows from Heaven

A story of faith, hope, and love that created a family.

Artemesia Publishing
c/o Lynn Ellen Doxon
12101 Palomas NE
Albuquerque, NM 87122
505-821-2808

Name: _____

Address: _____

_____

Telephone: _____

Order a copy for friends, family, a member of your church, or anyone who you feel would be inspired by this story of faith, hope, and love.

Quantity		Price	Total
_____	Rainbows from Heaven, Hardback	$24.95	_____
_____	Rainbows from Heaven, Paperback	$14.95	_____
	Total Due:		_____

Thank you very much for your order. God Bless.

Visit us on the web at www.artemesiapublishing.com

Prayers by a Wounded Warrior

A collection of inspirational prayers written by Laura Barnhart.

From the introduction:
"Prayer is the greatest gift we offer our Creator and the greatest gift He offers us. Through prayer, we join in a sacred union with God.

This is a collection of prayers for our hearts and minds, relationships, bodies, vocation, and the world. If your brow is furrowed with worry, fear or despair, may these prayers offer comfort, encouragement and healing. It is my hope that these prayers will soften your journey, make it easier and more gentle. If this is a time of celebration and things are going well, I join with you in prayers of gratitude, happiness and joy. May laughter fill your heart and spill over for all of us to share."

Prayers by a Wounded Warrior
By Laura Barnhart
ISBN: 1-932926-31-3